DEVELOPING LANGUAGE
COMPREHENSION
USING
MULTISENSORY ACTIVITIES

Marilyn M. Toomey

Illustrated by
Will Harney

CIRCUIT PUBLICATIONS, Inc.

Maplewood, New Jersey

Copyright © 2005
by Circuit Publications, Inc.
PO Box 1388
Maplewood, NJ 07040

09 08 07 06 05 TS 5 4 3 2 1

ISBN: 0-923573-50-X

Printed in the United States of America.

Table of Contents

Introduction

The ability to comprehend language, spoken or printed, is one of the most important components of cognitive and intellectual development. Comprehending language means grasping meaning and remembering what's heard or read. Verbal information along with life experiences, impressions and images is what makes up one's store of knowledge.

We call upon the comprehension process when we are trying to learn something. We listen or read using specific skills to learn. We work to understand the meaning of spoken or written information by drawing upon prior knowledge to help. We identify what is important and carry these important points along as we continue to process the speech/text and routinely summarize the information. We construct mental images of the ideas that the speech or text represent. We continuously monitor our comprehension, clarifying what we do not understand or what does not seem to fit. We then incorporate this new information into our store of knowledge. Comprehension is a very active process! Though we might not be conscious of these mental operations they are in full force as we work to comprehend and remember. Comprehension does not "just happen" - information does not simply "sink in" as we often suggest.

Many of our language impaired students do not treat comprehension as an active process and use strategies to understand and remember what they've heard or read. This book suggests a technique to help students work to understand and remember verbal information. Using three senses, **sight**, **hearing** and **touch**, students are guided to identify key information and to retain a visual image of an event.

These suggested activities make students aware that they must work in order to comprehend and remember. Here students are directed to use three senses to comprehend and remember an event. They **listen** to you tell them about the event while **looking** at a corresponding picture and actively identifying key points (**point to/touch**) of the event. Tasks such as this should help them learn to comprehend and remember information by actively participating. Students are led to build mental pictures of spoken or printed information, a most important aspect of comprehension and memory.

Here's how it works. . .

The book consists of 40 different events. Each one depicts a point in time in the daily lives of members of two families. For each event a student **sees** a picture (background and characters in action), and **listens** to and watches the instructor simultaneously read the corresponding text and **point to/touch** key elements of the picture. The student is then asked to restate the text-to "tell what is happening in the picture," as he or she points to/touches the key points in the picture. Following this, he or she answers questions while looking at the picture. Finally, the student is shown the setting only and asked questions. Three different sets of questions are keyed to each event. Within these three sets questions might be repeated using varied vocabulary or syntax, some including more challenging mental operations.

The characters (introduced on Page vii) are constant throughout the 40 units. Clues (generally the significant points of the event) are provided to help students recall information needed to answer questions in the final step of each unit.

Will and I hope that this book helps as speech/language pathologists work to help our students more readily develop and improve comprehension, a major building block in their intellectual development.

Marilyn

References:

Presley, M. (2002). *Reading instruction that works the case for balanced teaching.* New York: The Guilford Press.

Block, S.S., (2003). *Best Practices in Comprehension Instruction.* In L.M. Morrow, H.B. Gambrell, Michael Presley (Eds.) Best practices in literacy instruction (pp 111-126). New York: The Guilford Press.

Instructions for using *Developing Language Comprehension Using Multisensory Activities*

The activities for each of these 40 units is presented on three pages, an *Instructor Page* presenting step-by-step instructions is first. Next is *Picture #1*, a full page picture, followed by *Picture #2* which shows the setting only and individual picture clues. Following is an example of one of the units and an explanation of each step of the activity (Unit 19, Pages 55-57).

The goal of these activities is a student's active participation in comprehension tasks. Any portion of your presentation can be altered or simplified to best suit your student's learning style.

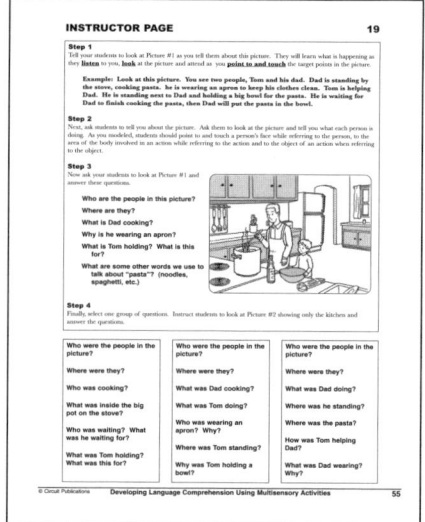

**Instructor Page
step-by-step instructions
for presentation**

Step 1

Copy the *Instructor Page* for your reference before beginning the activities in each unit. Instruct your student to **look at** *Picture #1*, the full page picture as you tell what's happening in the picture. A sample of the text that you might present is found in the *Example*. As you speak, your student should look at the picture and watch as you **point to/touch** key points in the picture.

Example: "Look at this picture. You see two people, Tom (point to Tom's face) and his dad (point to Dad's face). Dad (point to Dad) is cooking pasta (point to the pasta and the pot on the stove). He is wearing an apron (point to Dad's apron) to keep his clothes clean. Tom (point to Tom's face) is helping Dad (point to Dad), He (point to Tom) is standing next to Dad and holding a big bowl (point to Tom's hands on the bowl). He (point to Tom) is waiting for Dad to finish cooking the pasta (point to Dad, then to the pasta). Then Dad (point to Dad) will put the pasta (point to the pasta) in the bowl (point to the bowl)."

Step 2

Ask your student again to look at *Picture #1* (showing the characters in the setting) and tell **you** about the picture. Ask him or her to **look** at the picture and **tell** you what each person is doing along with other information about the event. As you modeled, the student should **point to and touch** a person's face while referring to the person, to the area of the body involved in the action while referring to the action and to the object of the action when referring to the object. Repeat, alter or simplify your presentation of the text as needed to compliment your student's needs.

**Picture #1
shows setting and characters**

Step 3

Instruct your student to look at *Picture #1* as a reference in answering questions in *Step 3*. This will help develop the concept and practice of using mental images to comprehend language. Help students by directing them to **point to and touch** significant points in the picture. Offer support as needed to evoke the answers.

Step 4

Finally, choose one set of questions and instruct your student to look at *Picture #2* (showing only the setting) and answer these questions. Here students must recall and restate information. This activity simulates the practice of answering questions following a story or expository passage. Clues are shown below *Picture #2*. These clues should help students recall information presented in *Step 1* by stimulating the memory of *Picture #1* where both setting and characters were shown.

Repeat earlier steps as needed until your student succeeds. *Step 4* in each unit presents three sets of questions. Choose one set at a time. Questions among the sets are often similar, varying only in vocabulary or syntax. Some could include inference or verbal reasoning. Note, it might be helpful to review the questions in *Step 4* before delivering your presentation in *Step 1* then adapt your presentation to suit your student's needs.

**Picture #2
shows setting only
and clues**

Developing Language Comprehension Using Multisensory Activities

These are the characters who you will meet as you work through this book.

Dad

Zoe

Tom

Mom

Luke

Dad

Liz

Ben

Mom

Champ

Cara

Step 1

Tell your students to look at Picture #1 as you tell them about this picture. They will learn what is happening as they **listen** to you, **look** at the picture and attend as you **point to and touch** the target points in the picture.

> **Example: Look at this picture. You see two children, Zoe and her brother, Tom. They are playing in their yard. Tom is running. Zoe is jumping. She is jumping over a log.**

Step 2

Next, ask students to tell you about the picture. Ask them to look at the picture and tell you what each person is doing. As you modeled, students should point to and touch a person's face while referring to the person and to the area of the body involved in an action while referring to the action.

Step 3

Now ask your students to look at Picture #1 and answer these questions.

Who are the children in this picture?

Where are Tom and Zoe?

Is Zoe jumping?

Is Tom jumping too?

Zoe is jumping over something. What is it?

Step 4

Finally, select one group of questions. Instruct students to look at Picture #2 showing only the yard and answer the questions.

Name the children who were in the picture. **Where were they?** **Was Tom jumping?** **Was Zoe running?** **What was Tom doing?** **Zoe was jumping over something. What was this?**	**Who were the children in the picture?** **Where were these children?** **What was Tom doing?** **What was Zoe doing?** **Was Zoe jumping over a puddle?**	**How many children were in the picture?** **Who were they?** **Where were these children?** **Who was jumping?** **Who was running?** **Was someone walking?**

Developing Language Comprehension Using Multisensory Activities
Unit 1 - Picture #1

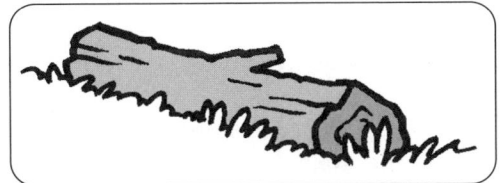

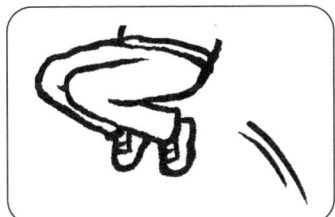

Step 1

Tell your students to look at Picture #1 as you tell them about this picture. They will learn what is happening as they **listen** to you, **look** at the picture and attend as you **point to and touch** the target points in the picture.

> **Example: Look at this picture. You see two children, Ben, and his sister, Liz. They are having fun outside. They are at a playground. Ben is swinging. Liz is sliding. She is going down the slide.**

Step 2

Next, ask students to tell you about the picture. Ask them to look at the picture and tell you what each person is doing. As you modeled, students should point to and touch a person's face while referring to the person and to the area of the body involved in an action while referring to the action.

Step 3

Now ask your students to look at Picture #1 and answer these questions.

Who are the children in this picture?

Where are Liz and Ben?

What is Liz doing?

What is Ben doing?

Step 4

Finally, select one group of questions. Instruct students to look at Picture #2 showing only the playground and answer the questions.

Name the children who were in this picture. **Where were Liz and Ben?** **Who was sliding?** **Who was swinging?** **In the picture was Liz going up or down? How do you know?**	**Tell me about the children who you saw in the picture. Who were they?** **Where were Liz and Ben?** **What was Ben doing?** **What was Liz doing?** **Was someone going down some stairs?**	**Who were the children in the picture?** **Where were these children?** **Was someone sliding? Who?** **Was someone climbing?** **Who was swinging?**

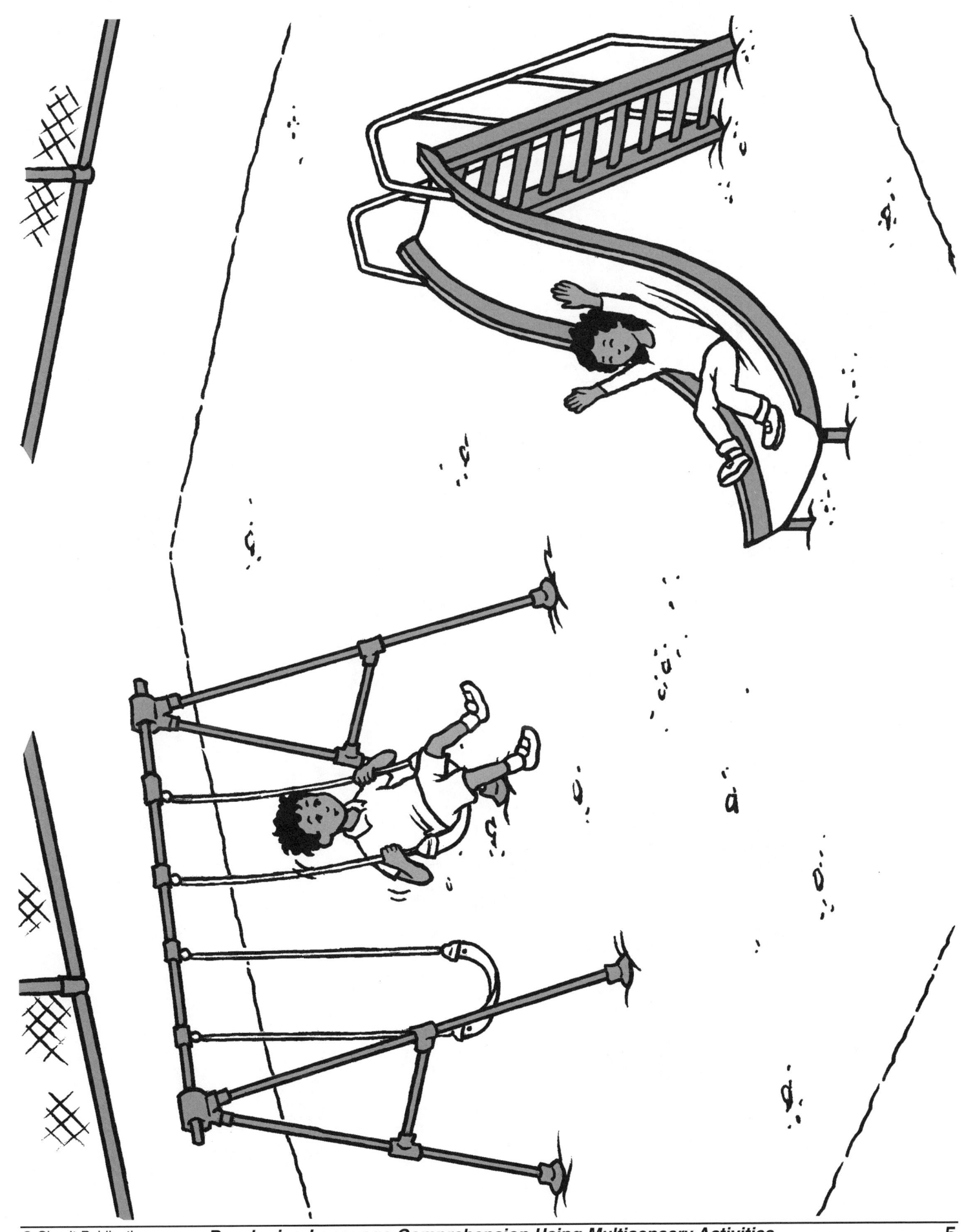

Developing Language Comprehension Using Multisensory Activities
Unit 2 - Picture #1

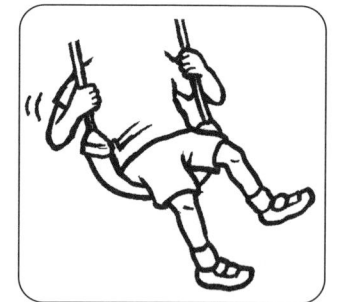

Developing Language Comprehension Using Multisensory Activities
Unit 2 - Picture #2 & Clues

Step 1

Tell your students to look at Picture #1 as you tell them about this picture. They will learn what is happening as they **listen** to you, **look** at the picture and attend as you **point to and touch** the target points in the picture.

> **Example: Look at this picture. You see two children, Tom and Zoe. They are in their playroom. They have just finished putting their toys away. Their mom is helping them. They are very tired and ready to go to bed. They are wearing their pajamas. Tom is yawning. Zoe is stretching.**

Step 2

Next, ask students to tell you about the picture. Ask them to look at the picture and tell you what each person is doing. As you modeled, students should point to and touch a person's face while referring to the person, to the area of the body involved in an action while referring to the action and to the object of an action when referring to the object.

Step 3

Now ask your students to look at Picture #1 and answer these questions.

Who are the children in this picture?

Where are they?

Is anyone else in this picture?

What are the children wearing?

What is Zoe doing?

What is Tom doing?

These children have just finished doing something. What was this?

How do you think Tom and Zoe feel now?

Step 4

Finally, select one group of questions. Instruct students to look at Picture #2 showing only the playroom and answer the questions.

Who were the children in the picture?

What were they wearing?

Who else was in the picture?

Where were they?

Who was yawning?

Who was stretching?

What time of day do you think it was?

What would Tom and Zoe be doing very soon?

You saw two children in the picture. Who were they?

Were there any grown-ups in the picture?

What was Tom doing?

What was Zoe doing?

Were Tom and Zoe ready to play or to sleep? Why?

What time of day do you think it was? Why do you think so?

Who were the children in the picture?

Where were they?

What were they wearing?

What was Zoe doing?

What was Tom doing?

How did Tom and Zoe probably feel?

Who was helping Tom and Zoe?

Developing Language Comprehension Using Multisensory Activities
Unit 3 - Picture #1

Step 1

Tell your students to look at Picture #1 as you tell them about this picture. They will learn what is happening as they **listen** to you, **look** at the picture and attend as you **point to and touch** the target points in the picture.

> **Example: Look at this picture. You see two people, Ben and his mom. They are in their kitchen. They are sitting at the kitchen table. Ben is talking to Mom. Mom is listening to him.**

Step 2

Next, ask students to tell you about the picture. Ask them to look at the picture and tell you what each person is doing. As you modeled, students should point to and touch a person's face while referring to the person, to the area of the body involved in an action while referring to the action and to the object of an action when referring to the object.

Step 3

Now ask your students to look at Picture #1 and answer these questions.

Who are the people in this picture?

Are they inside or outside?

In what room are they?

Someone is talking. Who is this?

Who is listening?

Speech bubble: "We played this new game at recess."

Step 4

Finally, select one group of questions. Instruct students to look at Picture #2 showing only the kitchen and answer the questions.

How many people were in the picture?	**Who was the child in the picture?**	**How many people were in the picture?**
Who were they?	**Who was the adult?**	**Who were they?**
Where were Ben and his mom?	**Where were they?**	**Where were they?**
Was Mom talking?	**Were they standing up?**	**Was someone listening? Who?**
Was Ben listening?	**What was Ben doing?**	**Was someone talking? Who?**
What do you think Ben might have been telling Mom?	**What was Mom doing?**	**What do you think Ben was telling Mom?**
	Was Liz in the picture too?	

> We played this new game at recest.

Developing Language Comprehension Using Multisensory Activities
Unit 4 - Picture #2 & Clues

Step 1

Tell your students to look at Picture #1 as you tell them about this picture. They will learn what is happening as they **listen** to you, **look** at the picture and attend as you **point to and touch** the target points in the picture.

> **Example: Look at this picture. You see two children who you know, Ben and his friend, Tom. They are on the school bus. They are on their way to school. Tom is sitting next to the window. Ben is sitting next to Tom. Tom is talking to Ben. He is probably telling Ben something that is funny because Ben is laughing.**

Step 2

Next, ask students to tell you about the picture. Ask them to look at the picture and tell you what each person is doing. As you modeled, students should point to and touch a person's face while referring to the person, to the area of the body involved in an action while referring to the action and to the object of an action when referring to the object.

Step 3

Now ask your students to look at Picture #1 and answer these questions.

Name the children you know who are in this picture?

Where are Tom and Ben?

Who is sitting next to the window?

Where is Ben sitting?

Is someone talking? Who?

What is Ben doing?

Why do you think that Ben is laughing?

Step 4

Finally, select one group of questions. Instruct students to look at Picture #2 showing only the school bus and answer the questions.

You saw two children who you know. Who were they?	**Who did you see in the picture?**	**Who did you see in the picture?**
Where were Tom and Ben?	**Where were they?**	**Where were Ben and Tom?**
Where were they going?	**Why were they on the bus?**	**Were they on their way home?**
Was Ben sitting next to the window?	**Were Ben and Tom standing up or sitting?**	**Was someone talking? Who?**
Who was Tom talking to?	**Who was talking?**	**Was someone laughing? Who?**
Who was listening to Tom?	**Who was listening?**	**Why was Ben probably laughing?**
	Who was laughing?	

Developing Language Comprehension Using Multisensory Activities
Unit 5 - Picture #1

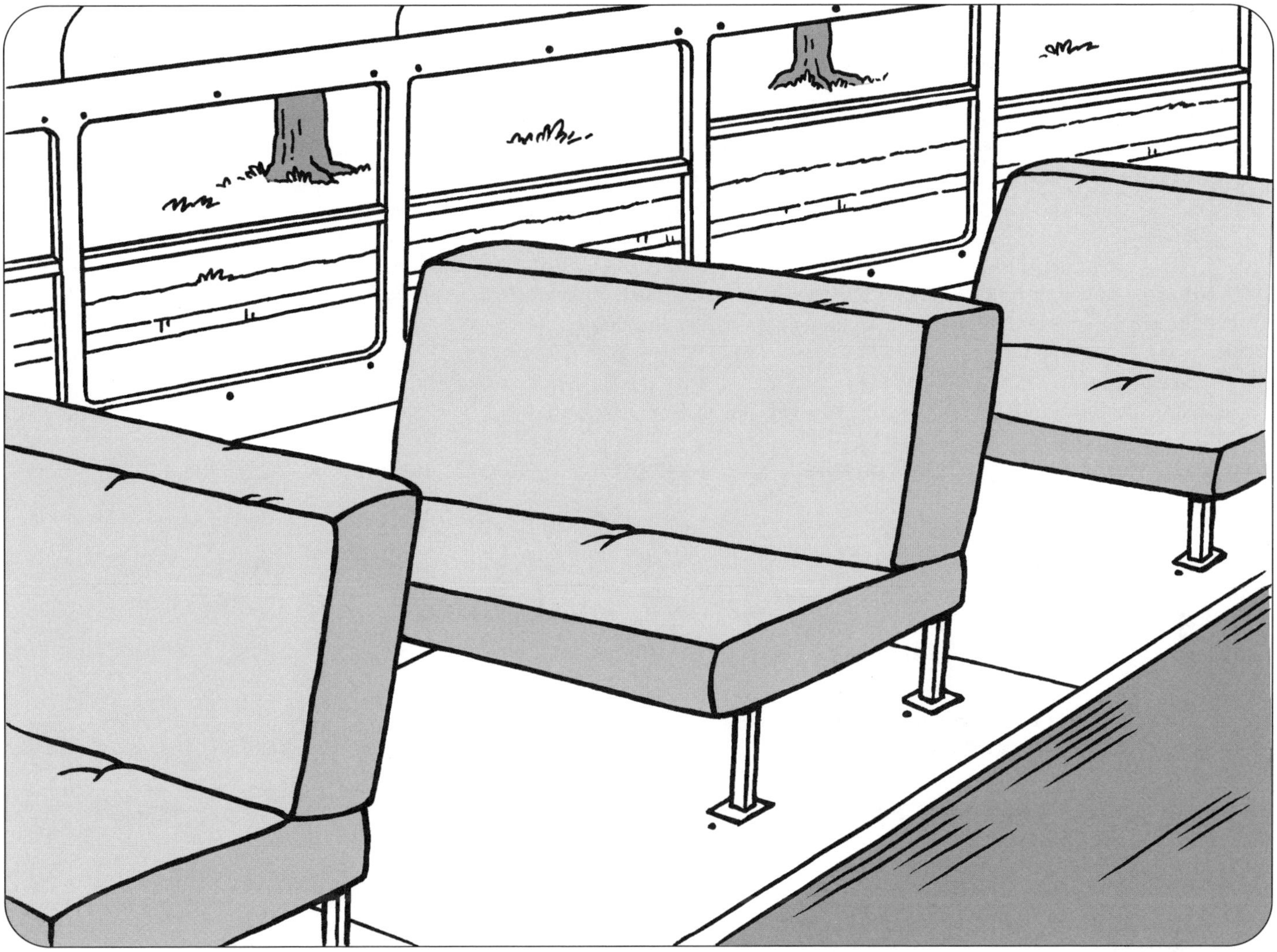

HA! HA! HA! HA!

He looked
so silly!

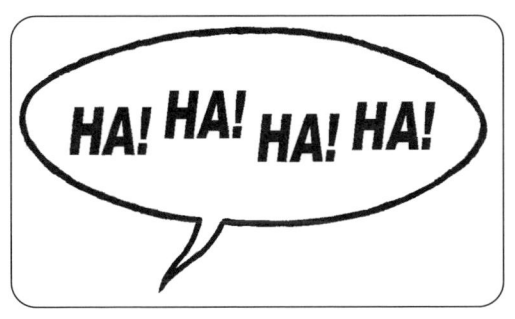

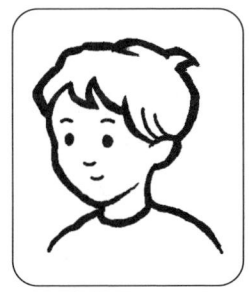

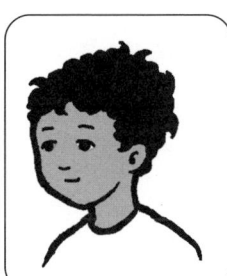

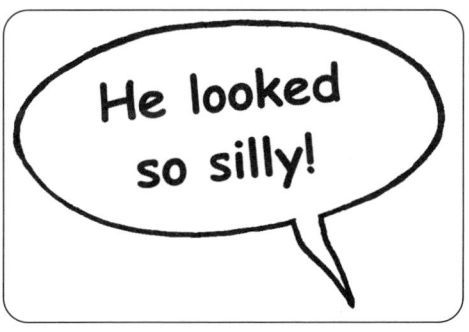

Step 1

Tell your students to look at Picture #1 as you tell them about this picture. They will learn what is happening as they **listen** to you, **look** at the picture and attend as you **point to and touch** the target points in the picture.

> **Example: Look at this picture. You see two boys, Ben and Tom. It is a cold winter day. The boys are at a frozen pond in the park. Ben is skating around the pond. He is having fun. Tom was having fun, but now he has a problem. He is falling down on the ice.**

Step 2

Next, ask students to tell you about the picture. Ask them to look at the picture and tell you what each person is doing. As you modeled, students should point to and touch a person's face while referring to the person and to the area of the body involved in an action while referring to the action.

Step 3

Now ask your students to look at Picture #1 and answer these questions.

Name the boys in this picture.

Where are these boys?

What kind of weather are they having?

One of the boys is having fun. Who?

One boy has a problem. Who is this? What is his problem?

Look at Tom's face. How do you think he feels?

Step 4

Finally, select one group of questions. Instruct students to look at Picture #2 showing only the pond and answer the questions.

Name the two boys that you saw in the picture.	Who were the children in the picture?	Name the boys who were in the picture?
Where were Tom and Ben?	Where were these boys?	Where were they?
What season was this? How do you know?	What season of the year was this? Why do you think so?	What kind of weather were they having?
Who was skating around the pond?	Someone was having a problem? Who? What was his problem?	Were both boys skating around the pond?
Who was not skating. Why not?	Was the ice pond in someone's back yard?	Who was probably enjoying himself?
		Remember how Tom's face looked? How did he probably feel?

Developing Language Comprehension Using Multisensory Activities
Unit 6 - Picture #1

The picture area contains a snowy scene with a tree on the left and a sign reading "DOVER POND".

Developing Language Comprehension Using Multisensory Activities
Unit 6 - Picture #2 & Clues

Step 1

Tell your students to look at Picture #1 as you tell them about this picture. They will learn what is happening as they **listen** to you, **look** at the picture and attend as you **point to and touch** the target points in the picture.

> **Example: Look at this picture. You see two characters, Liz and her dog, Champ. They are in their yard. Liz is standing. She is looking at Champ and smiling. Champ is sitting, looking at Liz.**

Step 2

Next, ask students to tell you about the picture. Ask them to look at the picture and tell you what each person is doing. As you modeled, students should point to and touch a person's face while referring to the person, to the area of the body involved in an action while referring to the action and to the object of an action when referring to the object.

Step 3

Now ask your students to look at Picture #1 and answer these questions.

Who is in this picture?

Where are Liz and her dog?

Liz is looking at Champ. Do you think she is happy to see Champ here?

Champ is looking at Liz. Is he standing up?

Is Liz standing or sitting?

Step 4

Finally, select one group of questions. Instruct students to look at Picture #2 showing only the yard and answer the questions.

Name the characters who were in the picture.	**Who were the characters in the picture?**	**Name the characters who were in the picture?**
Where were they?	**Where were they?**	**Where were they?**
Was Liz sitting down?	**What was Liz doing?**	**Who was standing up?**
Was Liz's mom or dad in the picture?	**What was Champ doing?**	**Who was smiling?**
Was Champ standing?	**One of these characters was smiling. Who?**	**Who was sitting?**
Was someone smiling? Who?	**Why do you think Liz was smiling at Champ?**	**Was someone lying down?**
Was Liz happy to see Champ? How do you know?		**Do you think Champ was in trouble?**

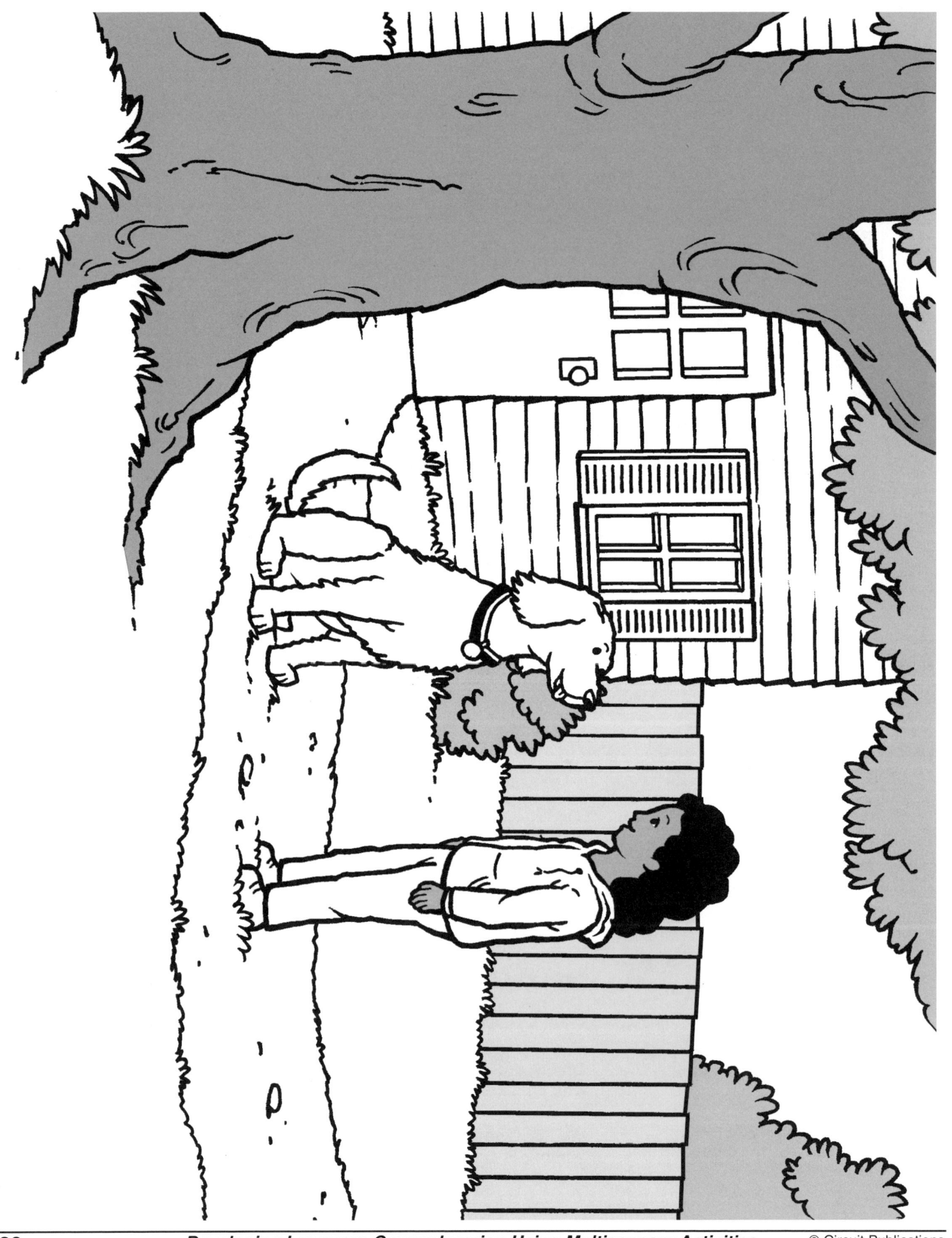

Developing Language Comprehension Using Multisensory Activities
Unit 7 - Picture #1

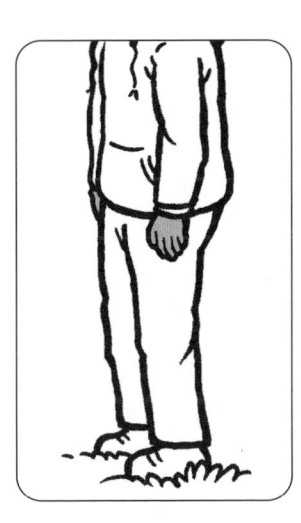

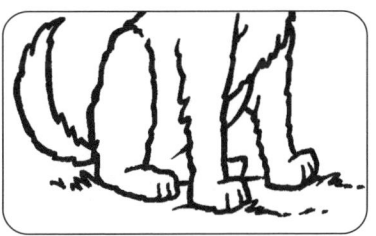

Step 1

Tell your students to look at Picture #1 as you tell them about this picture. They will learn what is happening as they **listen** to you, **look** at the picture and attend as you **point to and touch** the target points in the picture.

> **Example: Look at this picture. You see three children, Tom, Zoe, and their friend, Liz. They are in Tom and Zoe's yard. Tom is walking on a log. He is trying to balance himself so he will not fall off the log. He is holding his arms out to his sides to help him balance. Zoe and Liz are playing with a ball. Zoe is kicking the ball to Liz. Liz is ready to catch the ball.**

Step 2

Next, ask students to tell you about the picture. Ask them to look at the picture and tell you what each child is doing. As you modeled, students should point to and touch a child's face while referring to the child, to the area of the body involved in an action while referring to the action and to the object of an action when referring to the object.

Step 3

Now ask your students to look at Picture #1 and answer these questions.

Who are the children in this picture?

Where are they?

Two of the children are playing together. Who are they?

Who is kicking the ball?

Who is ready to catch the ball?

Tom is walking and trying to balance himself. What is he walking on?

Why is he holding his arms out to his sides?

Step 4

Finally, select one group of questions. Instruct students to look at Picture #2 showing only the yard and answer the questions.

Who were the children you saw in the picture?	**Name the children who were in the picture.**	**Who were the children in the picture?**
Where were they?	**Where were they?**	**Where were they?**
What was Tom doing?	**Zoe and Liz were playing together. What were they playing with?**	**What was Tom doing? Was this easy or difficult for him?**
What was Tom doing to balance himself on the log?	**Liz was ready to catch the ball. What was Zoe doing?**	**Who were the two children playing together?**
Who was kicking the ball?	**On what was Tom walking?**	**Who was kicking the ball?**
What was Liz doing?		**Who would catch it?**

Developing Language Comprehension Using Multisensory Activities
Unit 8 - Picture #1

Developing Language Comprehension Using Multisensory Activities
Unit 8 - Picture #2 & Clues

Step 1

Tell your students to look at Picture #1 as you tell them about this picture. They will learn what is happening as they **listen** to you, **look** at the picture and attend as you **point to and touch** the target points in the picture.

> **Example: Look at this picture. You see two children, Liz and Ben. They are having lunch at a restaurant with their mom. Ben is eating. He is eating his sandwich. Liz has finished eating her lunch. Now she is drinking her juice. Mom has also finished eating. Now she is holding a cup of hot tea.**

Step 2

Next, ask students to tell you about the picture. Ask them to look at the picture and tell you what each person is doing. As you modeled, students should point to and touch a person's face while referring to the person, to the area of the body involved in an action while referring to the action and to the object of an action when referring to the object.

Step 3

Now ask your students to look at Picture #1 and answer these questions.

Who are the people in this picture?

Where are they?

What time of day do you think it is here?

Is someone eating?

Who is holding something hot?

Who is drinking something that probably is not hot?

Step 4

Finally, select one group of questions. Instruct students to look at Picture #2 showing only the restaurant and answer the questions.

Who were the people in the picture?	Who were the people in the picture?	Who were the people in the picture?
Where were Liz, Ben and Mom?	Where were these people?	Where were they?
Who was with Ben and Liz?	Two people were finished eating their lunch. Who were they?	What time of day was this?
Who was eating?	Do you think it was early, late or in the middle of the day? Why?	Was anyone eating? Who?
Who was drinking?	Who had not yet finished eating?	Was someone drinking something that probably was not hot? Who?
Who was neither eating nor drinking?	What was Mom holding?	What was Mom holding?

Developing Language Comprehension Using Multisensory Activities
Unit 9 - Picture #1

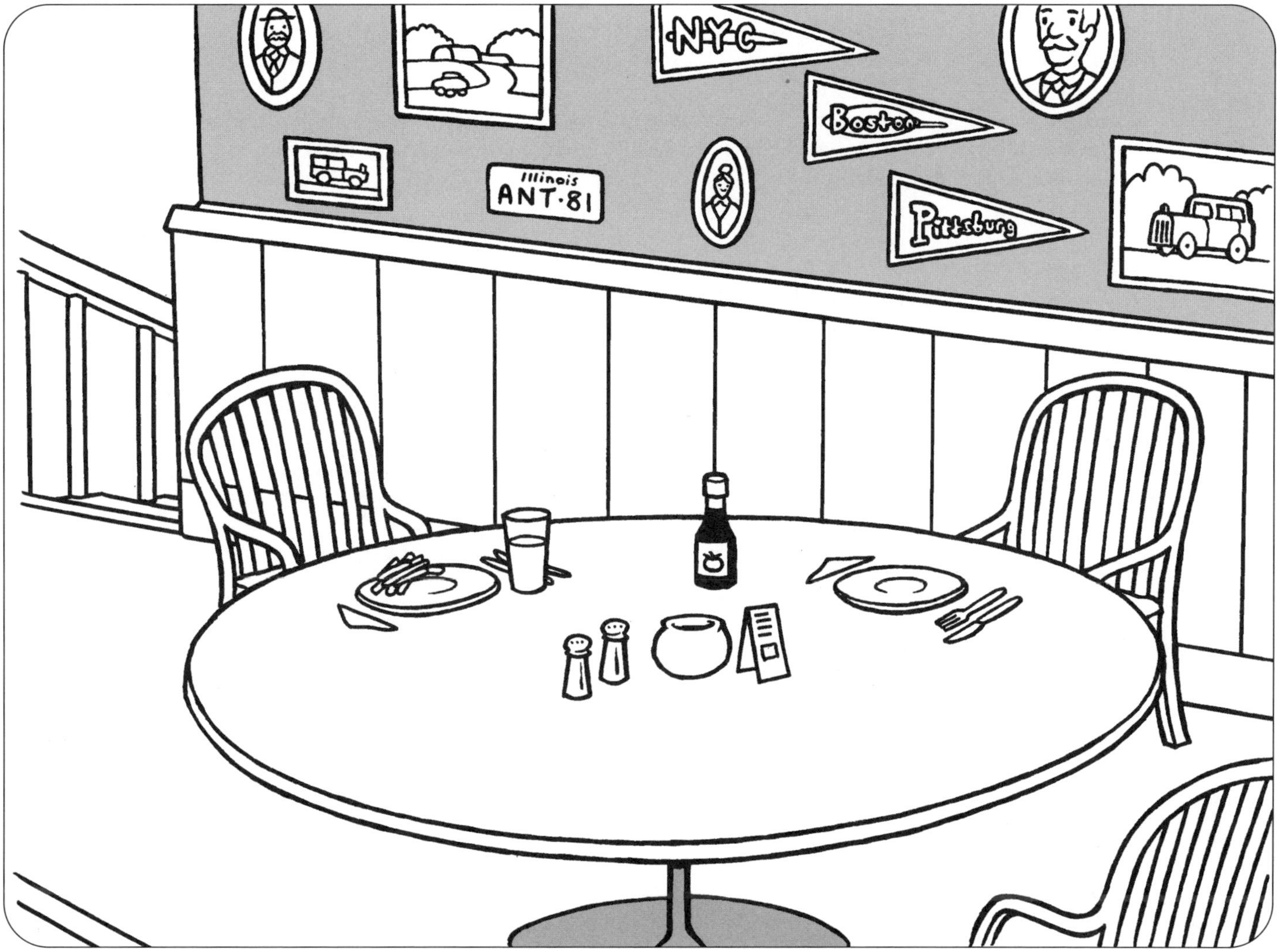
NYC
Boston
Illinois
ANT-81
Pittsburg

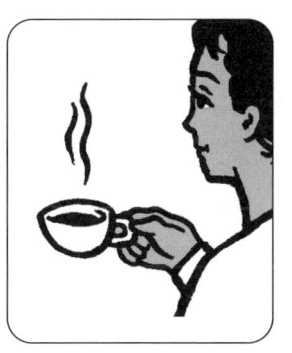

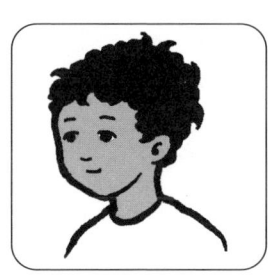

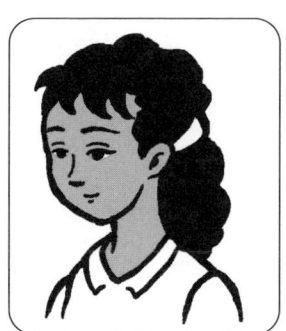

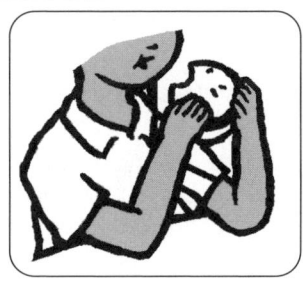

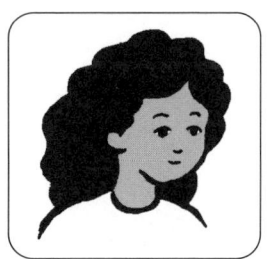

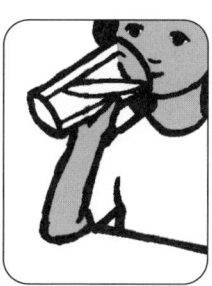

Step 1

Tell your students to look at Picture #1 as you tell them about this picture. They will learn what is happening as they **listen** to you, **look** at the picture and attend as you **point to and touch** the target points in the picture.

> **Example: Look at this picture. You see two animals, Champ and a squirrel. They are in Liz and Ben's yard. The squirrel is quickly climbing a tree. Champ is sitting near the tree. He is watching the squirrel.**

Step 2

Next, ask students to tell you about the picture. Ask them to look at the picture and tell you what each character is doing. As you modeled, students should point to and touch a character's face while referring to the character, to the area of the body involved in an action while referring to the action and to the object of an action when referring to the object.

Step 3

Now ask your students to look at Picture #1 and answer these questions.

Who is in this picture?

How many people do you see in this picture?

How many animals do you see? Who are they?

Where are these animals?

What is champ doing?

What is the squirrel doing?

Why do you think the squirrel is moving so fast?

Step 4

Finally, select one group of questions. Instruct students to look at Picture #2 showing only the yard and answer the questions.

Who were the characters in the picture?

Where were they?

What was the squirrel doing?

What was Champ doing?

Did Champ notice the squirrel?

How do you think the squirrel felt?

Who was in the picture?

Were these animals in the park?

What was the squirrel doing?

Did the squirrel know that Champ was watching him?

Do dogs like to chase squirrels?

What do you think Champ was thinking?

Who were the animals in the picture?

Where were they?

Was the squirrel running down the tree?

What was Champ doing?

Do you think the squirrel was happy that Champ was watching him? Why?

Developing Language Comprehension Using Multisensory Activities
Unit 10 - Picture #1

Developing Language Comprehension Using Multisensory Activities

Unit 10 - Picture #2 & Clues

Step 1

Tell your students to look at Picture #1 as you tell them about this picture. They will learn what is happening as they **listen** to you, **look** at the picture and attend as you **point to and touch** the target points in the picture.

> **Example: Look at this picture. You see two people, Ben and his dad. They are at a park. It is a nice warm day. Ben is riding his bike. He is riding his bike along a path in the park. Dad is swinging a golf club and hitting a golf ball. He is standing on the grass next to the bike path.**

Step 2

Next, ask students to tell you about the picture. Ask them to look at the picture and tell you what each person is doing. As you modeled, students should point to and touch a person's face while referring to the person, to the area of the body involved in an action while referring to the action and to the object of an action when referring to the object.

Step 3

Now ask your students to look at Picture #1 and answer these questions.

Who are the people in the picture?

Where are these people?

What is the weather like? Why do you think so?

Someone is riding something. Who is this? What is he riding?

Someone is standing on the grass. Who is this?

What is Dad swinging?

What is he hitting?

Step 4

Finally, select one group of questions. Instruct students to look at Picture #2 showing only the park and answer the questions.

Who were the people in the picture?	**Who was the boy in the picture?**	**Who were the people that you saw in the picture?**
Where were they?	**Who was the grown-up?**	**Where were these people?**
Was it warm or cold outside? Why do you think so?	**Where were they?**	**How do you know that it was a nice warm day outside?**
What was Ben riding?	**Who was riding something? What was he riding?**	**Did you see any animals in the picture?**
What was Dad hitting?	**Where was Ben riding his bike?**	**What was Ben doing?**
Who was on the path?	**What was Dad doing?**	**Was Dad hitting a golf ball in the woods?**
Who was standing on the grass?	**What season do you think it was?**	**Why is it better to hit golf balls on grass at a park than in the woods?**

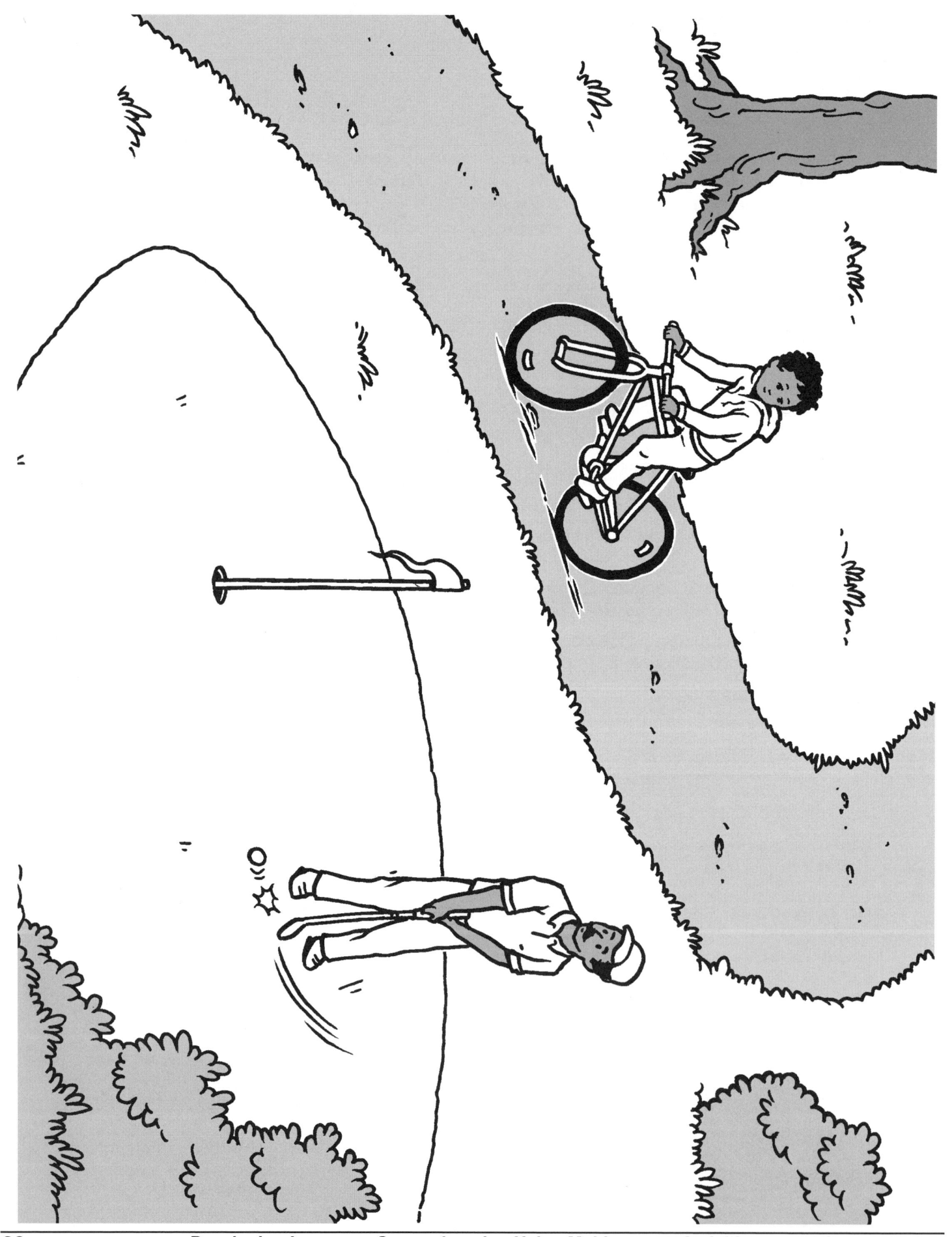

Developing Language Comprehension Using Multisensory Activities
Unit 11 - Picture #1

Step 1

Tell your students to look at Picture #1 as you tell them about this picture. They will learn what is happening as they **listen** to you, **look** at the picture and attend as you **point to and touch** the target points in the picture.

> **Example: Look at this picture. You see two children, Liz and her brother, Ben. They are at the beach. It is a nice warm day. Liz is kneeling in the sand. She is building a castle with sand. Ben is running on the beach. He is holding a string and flying a kite.**

Step 2

Next, ask students to tell you about the picture. Ask them to look at the picture and tell you what each child is doing. As you modeled, students should point to and touch a child's face while referring to the child, to the area of the body involved in an action while referring to the action and to the object of an action when referring to the object.

Step 3

Now ask your students to look at Picture #1 and answer these questions.

Who are the children in this picture?

Where are they?

Do you think it is a warm or a cold day? Why do you think so?

Someone is running. Who is this?

What is Ben holding?

How is he making the kite fly?

Is Liz standing up?

What is Liz building?

Step 4

Finally, select one group of questions. Instruct students to look at Picture #2 showing only the beach and answer the questions.

Who were the children in the picture? **Where were they?** **Why do you think it was a warm day?** **What was Liz building?** **What was Ben holding?** **What was tied to the string that Ben was holding?**	**How many children did you see in the picture? Who were they?** **Were they in their yard?** **Who was running? What else was this child doing?** **Who was kneeling? What else was this child doing?** **Was Tom running in the water?** **What was Liz's castle made of?**	**Name the children who were in the picture.** **Where were they?** **Why do you think it was not a cold day?** **Was someone swimming?** **Why was Ben running?** **What is Liz doing?** **What do you think would have happened if the water covered Liz's sand castle?**

Developing Language Comprehension Using Multisensory Activities
Unit 12 - Picture #1

Developing Language Comprehension Using Multisensory Activities

Unit 12 - Picture #2 & Clues

Step 1

Tell your students to look at Picture #1 as you tell them about this picture. They will learn what is happening as they **listen** to you, **look** at the picture and attend as you **point to and touch** the target points in the picture.

Example: Look at this picture. You see two people, Zoe and her mom. They are working in their garden on a warm spring day. Mom is kneeling down planting vegetable seeds. The seeds will grow into plants. The family will enjoy eating the vegetables from these plants. Zoe is working in the garden too. She is holding a sprinkling can full of water and watering flowers.

Step 2

Next, ask students to tell you about the picture. Ask them to look at the picture and tell you what each person is doing. As you modeled, students should point to and touch a person's face while referring to the person, to the area of the body involved in an action while referring to the action and to the object of an action when referring to the object.

Step 3

Now ask your students to look at Picture #1 and answer these questions.

Who are the two people in this picture?

Where are they?

What season is this?

What is Mom planting?

What will happen to these seeds?

What is Zoe holding?

What is she doing?

Step 4

Finally, select one group of questions. Instruct students to look at Picture #2 showing only the garden and answer the questions.

Who were the people in the picture?	Who were the people in the picture?	Who were the people in the picture?
Where were they?	Where were they?	Where were these people?
Who was planting something? What was this?	Who was kneeling? Why was she kneeling?	What season was this?
What was Zoe doing?	What was Zoe doing?	What was Mom doing?
What was she holding?	What would happen to the seeds that Mom was planting?	Why do people plant vegetable seeds?
	Why do flowers need water?	Will Mom's vegetable plants need water? Why?

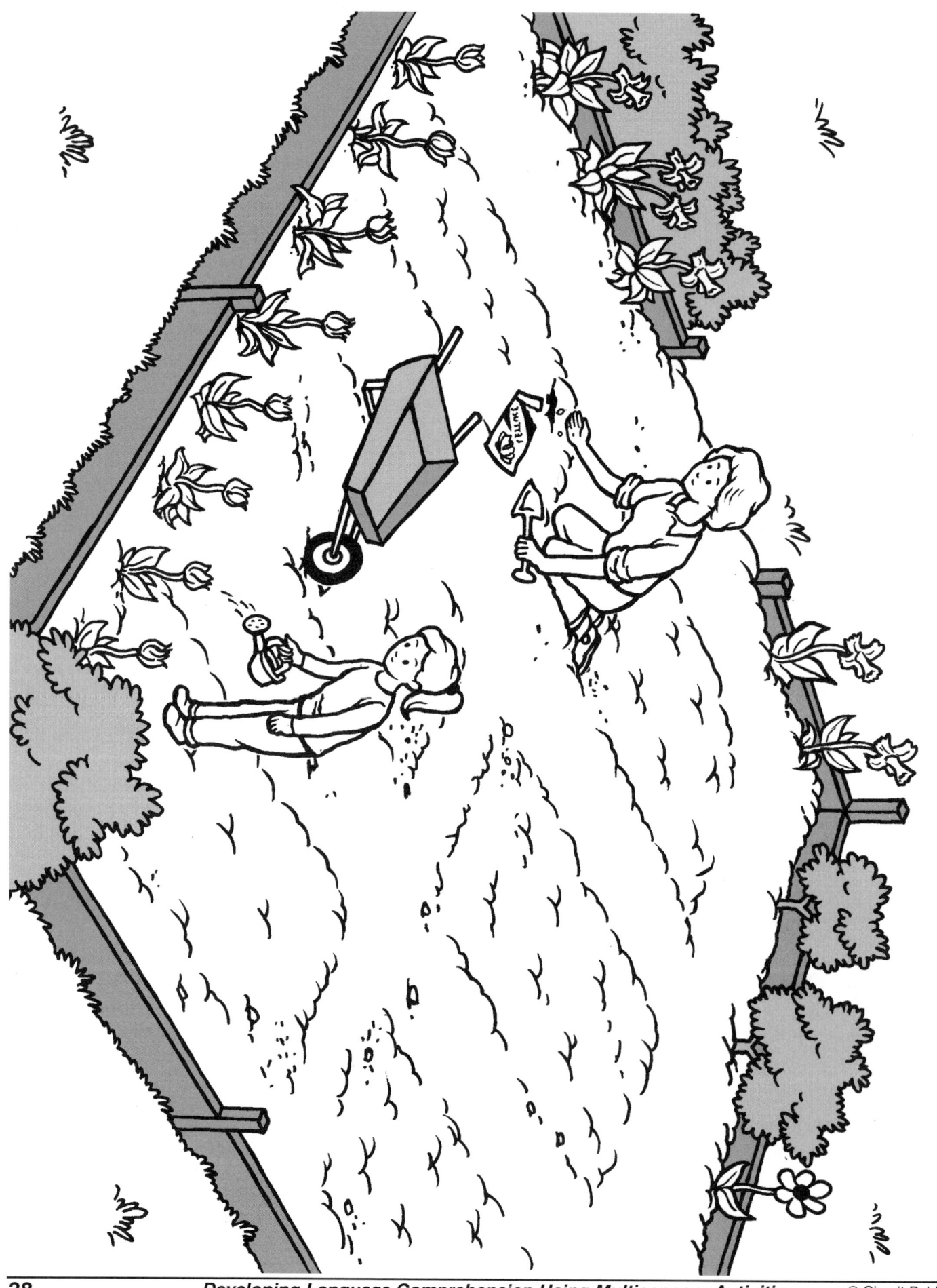

Developing Language Comprehension Using Multisensory Activities

Unit 13 - Picture #1

LETTUCE

Seeds

Developing Language Comprehension Using Multisensory Activities
Unit 13 - Picture #2 & Clues

Step 1

Tell your students to look at Picture #1 as you tell them about this picture. They will learn what is happening as they **listen** to you, **look** at the picture and attend as you **point to and touch** the target points in the picture.

    Example: Look at this picture. You see two people, Ben and his dad. They are standing at the bus stop. It is a rainy day. Dad is holding an umbrella up over Ben and himself. Ben is reading a sign.

Step 2

Next, ask students to tell you about the picture. Ask them to look at the picture and tell you what each person is doing. As you modeled, students should point to and touch a person's face while referring to the person, to the area of the body involved in an action while referring to the action and to the object of an action when referring to the object.

Step 3

Now ask your students to look at Picture #1 and answer these questions.

Who are the people in this picture?

Where are they?

What kind of weather are they having?

Who is holding something? What is this?

Why do you think Ben and his dad need an umbrella?

Who is reading something? What is he reading?

What is on the sign?

Step 4

Finally, select one group of questions. Instruct students to look at Picture #2 showing only the bus stop and answer the questions.

Who were the people in the picture?	Who were the people in the picture?	Who were the people in the picture?
Where were they?	Where were these people?	Where were they?
Was it warm and sunny outside?	What was Ben reading?	What was the weather like outside?
Who was reading a sign?	Who was holding an umbrella?	What was Ben doing?
What was Dad holding?	Were Ben and Dad sitting down?	What was Dad doing?
Was the umbrella opened or closed?	Why did Ben and his dad need an umbrella?	Were Ben and Dad getting wet in the rain? Why?

Developing Language Comprehension Using Multisensory Activities
Unit 14 - Picture #1

Developing Language Comprehension Using Multisensory Activities
Unit 14 - Picture #2 & Clues

Step 1

Tell your students to look at Picture #1 as you tell them about this picture. They will learn what is happening as they <u>listen</u> to you, **look** at the picture and attend as you **point to and touch** the target points in the picture.

> **Example: Look at this picture. You see two children, Tom and Zoe. They are playing in the snow in their yard. Zoe is making a snowman. She is rolling a very big snowball. The big snowball will become the snowman's head. Tom just finished making a snow angel. He is standing and looking down at the snow angel that he made.**

Step 2

Next, ask students to tell you about the picture. Ask them to look at the picture and tell you what each child is doing. As you modeled, students should point to and touch a child's face while referring to the child, to the area of the body involved in an action while referring to the action and to the object of an action when referring to the object.

Step 3

Now ask your students to look at Picture #1 and answer these questions.

Who are the children in this picture?

Where are they?

Is it warm or cold outside? Why do you think so?

Tom just finished making something. What is this?

How do you think he made this angel?

What will happen with the big snowball Zoe is rolling?

Step 4

Finally, select one group of questions. Instruct students to look at Picture #2 showing only the yard and answer the questions.

Who were the children in the picture? **Where were they?** **What time of year do you think it was? Why?** **What was Tom looking at?** **Where had this angel come from?** **What was Zoe rolling? What was this for?**	**Name the children who were in the picture.** **Where were they?** **Who had finished making something? What was this?** **Who had not yet finished making something? What would this become?** **What was Tom doing in the picture?**	**Who were the children in the picture?** **Where were these children?** **What season was this?** **How do you think Tom had made his snow angel?** **Who was rolling a big snowball? Why?** **How would Zoe probably put the snowman's head on?**

Developing Language Comprehension Using Multisensory Activities
Unit 15 - Picture #1

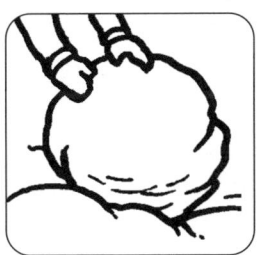

Step 1

Tell your students to look at Picture #1 as you tell them about this picture. They will learn what is happening as they **listen** to you, **look** at the picture and attend as you **point to and touch** the target points in the picture.

> **Example: Look at this picture. You see two people, Luke and his mom. They are in the garden. You also see a rabbit. The rabbit is eating some lettuce. Mom is pulling weeds out of the ground. She does not see the rabbit. She would not be happy to see the rabbit eating the lettuce! Luke sees the rabbit. He is watching the rabbit eat the lettuce.**

Step 2

Next, ask students to tell you about the picture. Ask them to look at the picture and tell you what each character is doing. As you modeled, students should point to and touch a character's face while referring to the character, to the area of the body involved in an action while referring to the action and to the object of an action when referring to the object.

Step 3

Now ask your students to look at Picture #1 and answer these questions.

Who are the people in this picture?

Where are they?

Who else is in the picture?

What is Mom doing?

What is the rabbit doing?

What is Luke doing?

Do you think Mom knows the rabbit is in the garden?

Step 4

Finally, select one group of questions. Instruct students to look at Picture #2 showing only the garden and answer the questions.

Who were the people that you saw in the picture? **Where were they?** **What was Mom pulling out of the ground?** **What was Luke watching?** **What was the rabbit doing?** **Was Mom watching the rabbit too?** **Would she be happy to see the rabbit eating lettuce?**	**Who were the people in the picture?** **Where were they?** **Who was pulling weeds out of the ground?** **What was Luke doing?** **What kind of animal was in the garden?** **Who was eating something? What?**	**Who were the people in the picture?** **Where were they?** **What was Mom doing?** **Was Mom standing up?** **What was Luke doing?** **Who was eating the lettuce?** **Why do you think Mom would not want the rabbit to eat the lettuce?**

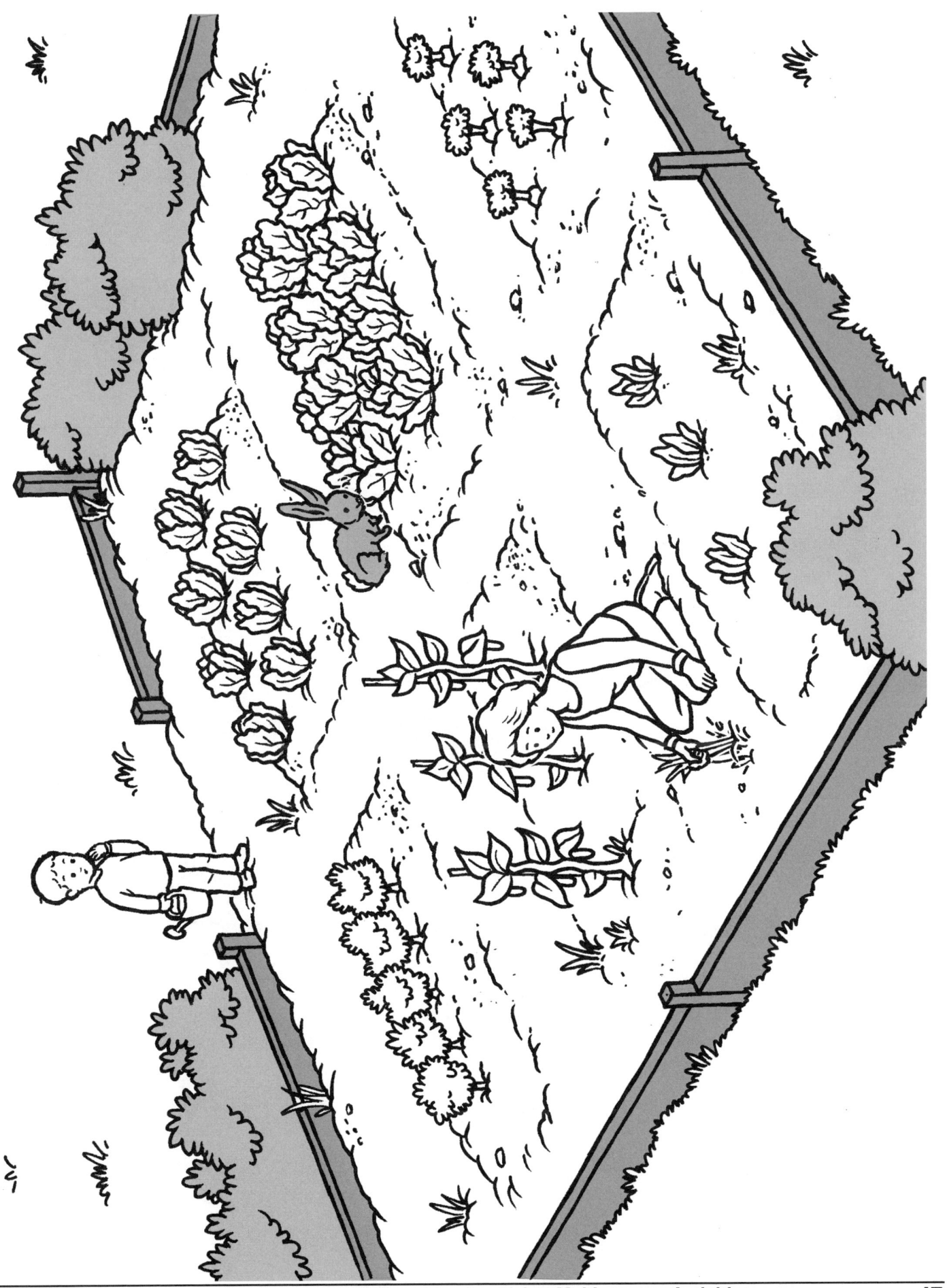

Developing Language Comprehension Using Multisensory Activities 47

Unit 16 - Picture #1

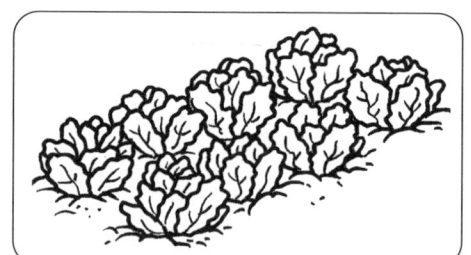

Developing Language Comprehension Using Multisensory Activities
Unit 16 - Picture #2 & Clues

Step 1

Tell your students to look at Picture #1 as you tell them about this picture. They will learn what is happening as they **listen** to you, **look** at the picture and attend as you **point to and touch** the target points in the picture.

> **Example: Look at this picture. You see two people, Liz and her dad. They are in a grocery store. They are in the produce department of the store where fruits and vegetables are found. Dad is pushing their shopping cart. He is looking at the fruit deciding what kinds of fruit to choose. Liz decided that she wants a pineapple. She is holding the pineapple that she chose.**

Step 2

Next, ask students to tell you about the picture. Ask them to look at the picture and tell you what each person is doing. As you modeled, students should point to and touch a person's face while referring to the person, to the area of the body involved in an action while referring to the action and to the object of an action when referring to the object.

Step 3

Now ask your students to look at Picture #1 and answer these questions.

    Who are the people who you see in this picture?

    Where are they?

    What is Dad pushing? What is he looking at?

    What has Liz chosen?

    Which kinds of foods are found in a store's produce department?

Step 4

Finally, select one group of questions. Instruct students to look at Picture #2 showing only the grocery store and answer the questions.

Who were the people in the picture? **In what kind of store were they?** **Who was deciding?** **Who had chosen something? What was this?** **What was Dad pushing?** **What was Liz doing?**	**Who were the people in the picture?** **In what department of the store were they? What is found in this department?** **What was Liz holding?** **Who was deciding what to choose?** **Who was pushing a shopping cart?**	**Who were the people in the picture?** **Where were they?** **Liz and Dad were choosing fruits to buy. Who had not yet chosen something?** **Why do you think Liz probably chose a pineapple?** **What would you select from the produce department?**

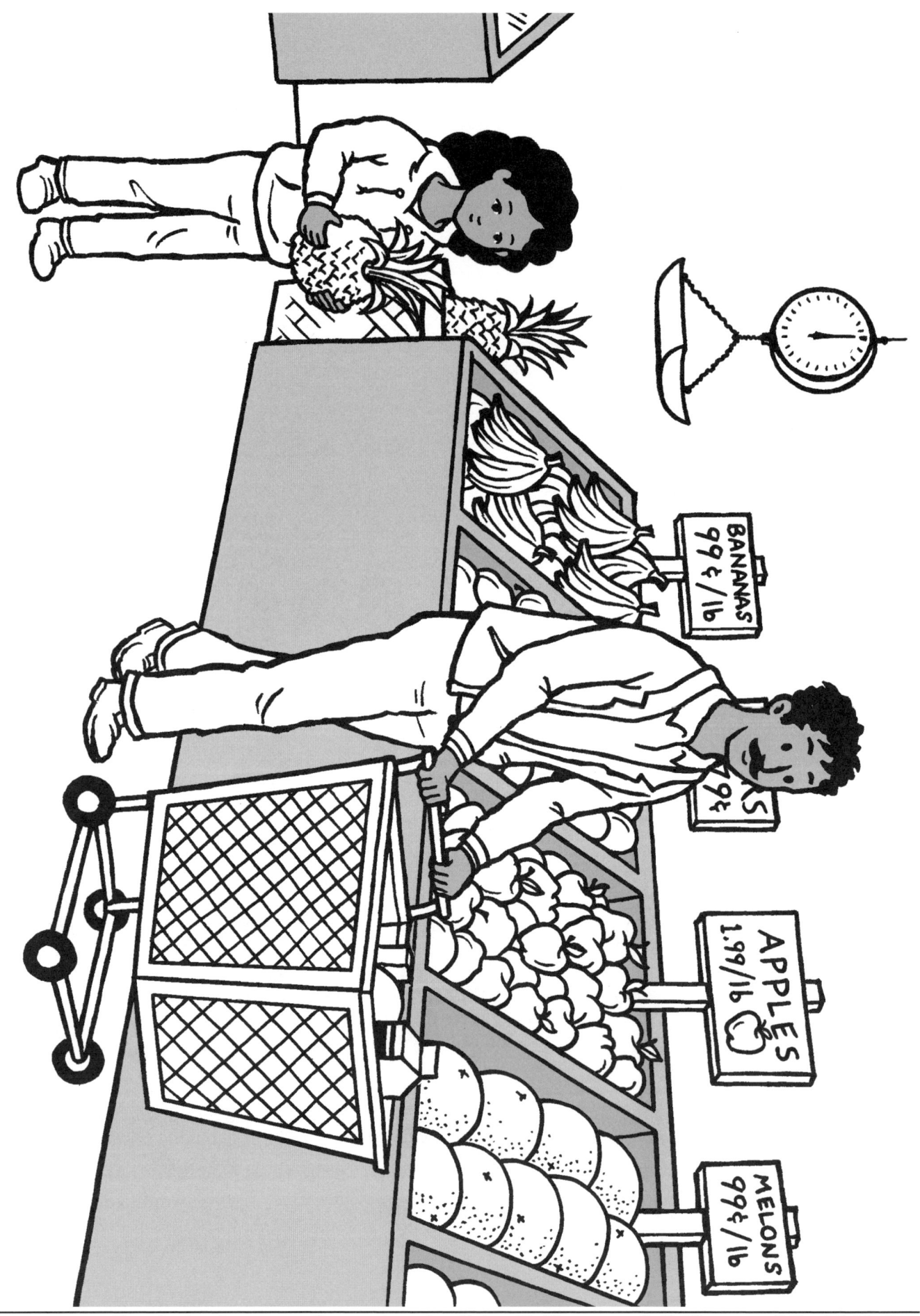

Developing Language Comprehension Using Multisensory Activities
Unit 17 - Picture #1

BANANAS
99¢/lb

PEARS
3/79¢

APPLES
1.99/lb

MELONS
99¢/lb

Step 1

Tell your students to look at Picture #1 as you tell them about this picture. They will learn what is happening as they **listen** to you, **look** at the picture and attend as you **point to and touch** the target points in the picture.

> **Example: Look at this picture. You see Luke with his mom and dad. They are in a clothing store. You also see a salesman. Dad has chosen a tie to buy. He has just given the salesman some money for the tie. The salesman will put this money in the cash register. Mom is standing behind Dad. She is waiting for the salesman to give Dad his tie. She is looking at her watch. Luke is standing behind Mom. He is waiting for Dad too.**

Step 2

Next, ask students to tell you about the picture. Ask them to look at the picture and tell you what each person is doing. As you modeled, students should point to and touch a person's face while referring to the person, to the area of the body involved in an action while referring to the action and to the object of an action when referring to the object.

Step 3

Now ask your students to look at Picture #1 and answer these questions.

You see four people in this picture. Who are they?

Where are these people?

What is Dad holding?

What is the salesman holding?

What is Mom looking at?

Why did Dad give money to the salesman?

Where is Luke standing?

Step 4

Finally, select one group of questions. Instruct students to look at Picture #2 showing only the clothing store and answer the questions.

Who were the four people in the picture?	**Who were the people in the picture?**	**Who were the people in the picture?**
Where were these people?	**Why were they at the clothing store?**	**Where were they?**
Someone had chosen something to buy. Who? What was chosen?	**What was Dad buying?**	**What was Dad holding?**
What was the salesman holding?	**Where was Mom standing?**	**What was the salesman holding?**
	What was she looking at?	**Where did the money belong?**
Two people were waiting. Who were they? Why were they waiting?	**Why was the salesman holding money?**	**Who was finding out what time it was?**
		Where is Luke standing?

Developing Language Comprehension Using Multisensory Activities
Unit 18 - Picture #1

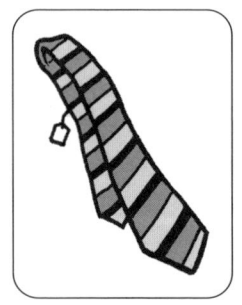

Developing Language Comprehension Using Multisensory Activities
Unit 18 - Picture #2 & Clues

Step 1

Tell your students to look at Picture #1 as you tell them about this picture. They will learn what is happening as they **listen** to you, **look** at the picture and attend as you **point to and touch** the target points in the picture.

> **Example: Look at this picture. You see two people, Tom and his dad. Dad is standing by the stove, cooking pasta. He is wearing an apron to keep his clothes clean. Tom is helping Dad. He is standing next to Dad and holding a big bowl for the pasta. He is waiting for Dad to finish cooking the pasta, then Dad will put the pasta in the bowl.**

Step 2

Next, ask students to tell you about the picture. Ask them to look at the picture and tell you what each person is doing. As you modeled, students should point to and touch a person's face while referring to the person, to the area of the body involved in an action while referring to the action and to the object of an action when referring to the object.

Step 3

Now ask your students to look at Picture #1 and answer these questions.

Who are the people in this picture?

Where are they?

What is Dad cooking?

Why is he wearing an apron?

What is Tom holding? What is this for?

What are some other words we use to talk about "pasta"? (noodles, spaghetti, etc.)

Step 4

Finally, select one group of questions. Instruct students to look at Picture #2 showing only the kitchen and answer the questions.

Who were the people in the picture?	Who were the people in the picture?	Who were the people in the picture?
Where were they?	Where were they?	Where were they?
Who was cooking?	What was Dad cooking?	What was Dad doing?
What was inside the big pot on the stove?	What was Tom doing?	Where was he standing?
Who was waiting? What was he waiting for?	Who was wearing an apron? Why?	Where was the pasta?
What was Tom holding? What was this for?	Where was Tom standing?	How was Tom helping Dad?
	Why was Tom holding a bowl?	What was Dad wearing? Why?

Developing Language Comprehension Using Multisensory Activities
Unit 19 - Picture #1

SPAGETTI

Developing Language Comprehension Using Multisensory Activities
Unit 19 - Picture #2 & Clues

Step 1

Tell your students to look at Picture #1 as you tell them about this picture. They will learn what is happening as they **listen** to you, **look** at the picture and attend as you **point to and touch** the target points in the picture.

> **Example: Look at this picture. You see two children, Liz and her friend, Zoe. They are in their classroom. The girls are sitting at a table and working together. They are working on a special project. They are making a model of a village in a place that is far away. Liz is painting. She is painting a picture of grass and trees and a road in the village. Zoe is cutting. She is making little huts like the homes where the people in this village live.**

Step 2

Next, ask students to tell you about the picture. Ask them to look at the picture and tell you what each child is doing. As you modeled, students should point to and touch a child's face while referring to the child, to the area of the body involved in an action while referring to the action and to the object of an action when referring to the object.

Step 3

Now ask your students to look at Picture #1 and answer these questions.

Who do you see in this picture?

Where are Liz and Zoe?

Is each girl working alone or are they working together?

What is their special project?

Is someone cutting? Who?

What is Liz painting?

How is a model of a village different from a real village?

Step 4

Finally, select one group of questions. Instruct students to look at Picture #2 showing only the classroom and answer the questions.

Who did you see in the picture?	**Who did you see in the picture?**	**Who did you see in the picture?**
Where were Zoe and Liz?	**Where were they?**	**Where were these girls?**
Where were they sitting?	**Were they working alone?**	**Were they working separately?**
What was the project the girls were working on?	**Were they making a model of a place close to their homes?**	**Were the girls making a model of a place, an animal or a machine?**
Was Zoe cutting?	**What was Zoe using?**	**What was Liz painting?**
Was Liz painting	**What was Liz using?**	**What was Zoe doing?**
Were these girls working alone or together?		**What do you think their model would look like when it was finished?**

Developing Language Comprehension Using Multisensory Activities
Unit 20 - Picture #1

Developing Language Comprehension Using Multisensory Activities
Unit 20 - Picture #2 & Clues

Step 1

Tell your students to look at Picture #1 as you tell them about this picture. They will learn what is happening as they **listen** to you, **look** at the picture and attend as you **point to and touch** the target points in the picture.

> **Example: Look at this picture. You see three people, Tom, his dad and a barber. They are at the barber shop. The barber is talking. He is telling Tom's dad about something that happened in town. Tom's dad is listening to the barber. Tom is sitting in the barber chair. He is ready for the barber to cut his hair. He is listening to the barber too.**

Step 2

Next, ask students to tell you about the picture. Ask them to look at the picture and tell you what each person is doing. As you modeled, students should point to and touch a person's face while referring to the person, to the area of the body involved in an action while referring to the action and to the object of an action when referring to the object.

Step 3

Now ask your students to look at Picture #1 and answer these questions.

I DON'T KNOW HOW THAT COULD HAVE HAPPENED.

Who are the people in this picture?

Where are these people?

Who is sitting?

Someone is talking. Who?

Two people are listening to the barber. Who are they?

Who is ready to get his hair cut?

What is the barber talking about?

Step 4

Finally, select one group of questions. Instruct students to look at Picture #2 showing only the barber shop and answer the questions.

Who were the people in the picture?	There were two grown-ups in the picture. Who were they?	There were three people in the picture. Who were they?
Where were they?		Where were these people?
Someone was ready to get his hair cut. Who?	Who else was in the picture?	Why do you think Tom and his dad came to the barber shop today?
Two people were standing. Who were they?	Where were these people?	Two people were standing. Who were they?
Was Tom's dad talking?	What was Tom's dad doing?	Who was talking?
Who was talking? What was he talking about?	What was the barber doing?	Two people were listening. Who were they?
Who was Tom listening to?	Where was Tom sitting?	
	Why was he sitting there?	

Developing Language Comprehension Using Multisensory Activities

Developing Language Comprehension Using Multisensory Activities
Unit 21 - Picture #1

Step 1

Tell your students to look at Picture #1 as you tell them about this picture. They will learn what is happening as they **listen** to you, **look** at the picture and attend as you **point to and touch** the target points in the picture.

> **Example: Look at this picture. You see two children, Luke and his friend, Cara. You also see their teacher. They are in their preschool classroom. Cara is working with blocks. She is building a tower with them. Luke is painting. He is painting a picture of a tree. Their teacher is talking to them. They are looking at their teacher and listening to her.**

Step 2

Next, ask students to tell you about the picture. Ask them to look at the picture and tell you what each person is doing. As you modeled, students should point to and touch a person's face while referring to the person, to the area of the body involved in an action while referring to the action and to the object of an action when referring to the object.

Step 3

Now ask your students to look at Picture #1 and answer these questions.

Name the children in this picture.

Is there a grown-up in the picture? Who is this?

Where are these people?

Someone is painting. Who?

What is Cara doing?

Someone is talking. Who is this?

Who is listening to the teacher?

Step 4

Finally, select one group of questions. Instruct students to look at Picture #2 showing only the preschool classroom and answer the questions.

Who were the people in the picture?	**There were three people in the picture. Who were they?**	**Name the children who were in the picture?**
Where were they?	**Where were these people?**	**Was there an adult in the picture? Who was this?**
Who was painting a picture?	**Who was building?**	**What was Cara working with? What was she building?**
Do you remember what Luke was painting?	**What was the teacher doing?**	**What was Luke working with? What was he painting?**
What was Cara doing?	**What was Luke doing?**	**Was their teacher painting too?**
What was the teacher doing?	**Were Luke and Cara looking out the window?**	**Were Cara and Luke paying attention to their teacher as she talked to them? How do you know?**
Was someone listening to the teacher? Who was listening?	**Was someone painting a picture of a horse?**	
	Was someone talking? Who?	

Developing Language Comprehension Using Multisensory Activities

Developing Language Comprehension Using Multisensory Activities
Unit 22 - Picture #2 & Clues

Step 1

Tell your students to look at Picture #1 as you tell them about this picture. They will learn what is happening as they **listen** to you, **look** at the picture and attend as you **point to and touch** the target points in the picture.

> **Example: Look at this picture. You see three characters, Ben, Liz and their dog, Champ. They are in the park on a cold winter day. Ben and Liz are skating on a frozen pond. Ben is skating across the pond. Liz is spinning around on her skates. Champ is digging in the snow near the pond.**

Step 2

Next, ask students to tell you about the picture. Ask them to look at the picture and tell you what each person is doing. As you modeled, students should point to and touch a person's face while referring to the person and to the area of the body involved in an action while referring to the action.

Step 3

Now ask your students to look at Picture #1 and answer these questions.

> Name the characters who are in this picture.
>
> Where are they.
>
> What kind of weather are they having?
>
> Who is spinning around?
>
> Who is skating across the pond?
>
> What is Champ doing?

Step 4

Finally, select one group of questions. Instruct students to look at Picture #2 showing only the frozen pond and answer the questions.

Who were the children in the picture?	Name the children and the dog who were in the picture?	Who were the characters in the picture?
Where were they?	Where were they?	Where were they?
Who else was there?	Was it warm or cold outside? How do you know?	What season was this?
What season of the year was it?	What was Ben doing?	How were the children dressed to keep warm?
Who was skating across the pond?	Was someone spinning?	Who was skating across the pond?
Who was digging in the snow?	Was someone falling down?	What was Liz doing?
Who was spinning around?	Was Champ digging in the mud?	What was Champ, doing?
Were there any grown-ups in the picture?		Was Champ wearing something special to keep warm? Why not?

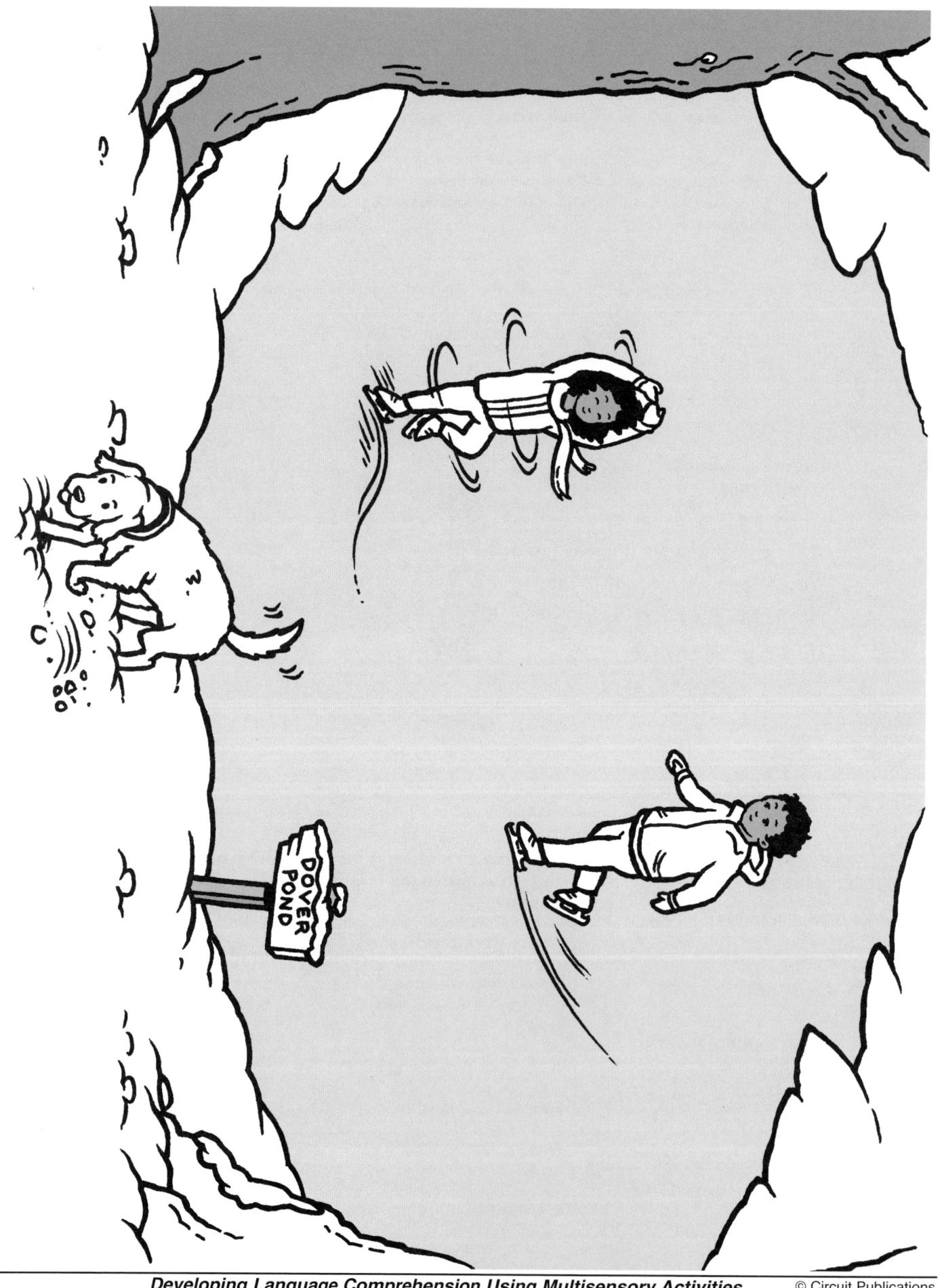

Developing Language Comprehension Using Multisensory Activities
Unit 23 - Picture #1

Step 1

Tell your students to look at Picture #1 as you tell them about this picture. They will learn what is happening as they **listen** to you, **look** at the picture and attend as you **point to and touch** the target points in the picture.

> **Example: Look at this picture. You see three children, Zoe, Liz and Zoe's little brother, Luke. They are at a playground. You also see their babysitter, Danielle. Liz is climbing up a ladder. Zoe is sliding down a slide. Zoe's brother, Luke is at the playground too. He is playing in the sandbox. He is pouring sand out of a pail. Danielle is at the playground with them. She is watching the children as they play. She is standing near Luke so she can watch him closely**

Step 2

Next, ask students to tell you about the picture. Ask them to look at the picture and tell you what each person is doing. As you modeled, students should point to and touch a person's face while referring to the person, to the area of the body involved in an action while referring to the action and to the object of an action when referring to the object.

Step 3

Now ask your students to look at Picture #1 and answer these questions.

Who are the people in this picture?

Where are they?

Someone is climbing. Who is this?

Who is sliding?

What is Luke pouring?

Why is Danielle, the babysitter, at the playground?

Step 4

Finally, select one group of questions. Instruct students to look at Picture #2 showing only the playground and answer the questions.

Who were the three children in the picture? **Was there someone else at the playground? Who was this?** **Where were they?** **What was Zoe doing?** **What was Liz climbing?** **Who was playing in the sandbox?** **What was Danielle, the babysitter, doing?**	**Who were the children you saw in the picture?** **Where were they?** **Who was climbing?** **Was Liz going up or down the slide?** **What was Luke holding? What was he doing with this?** **Why was Danielle at the playground with the children?**	**Name the children who were in the picture?** **Where was Luke playing?** **Was someone sliding? Who?** **Was someone climbing? Who?** **Where was Danielle standing? Why was she standing there?**

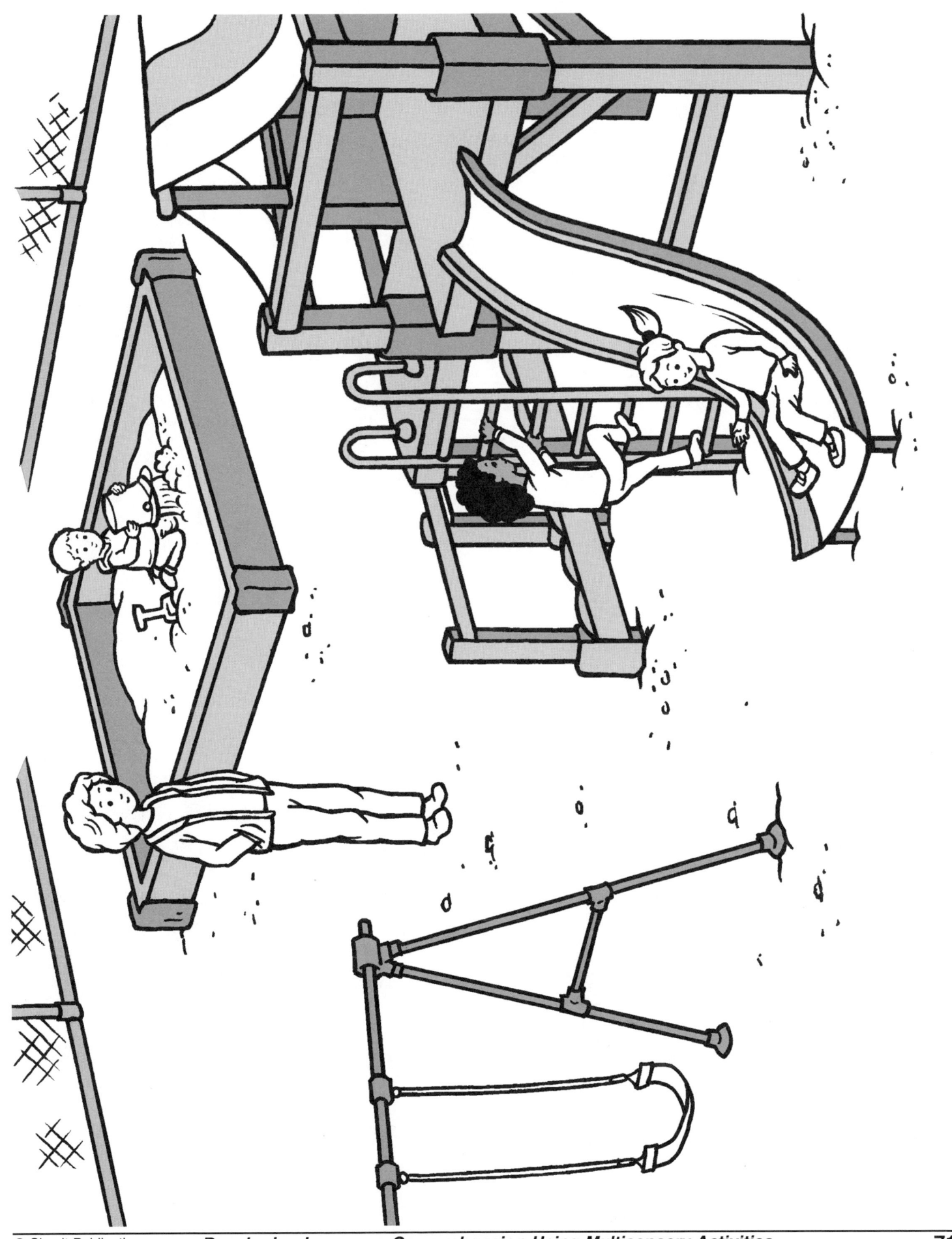

Developing Language Comprehension Using Multisensory Activities
Unit 24 - Picture #1

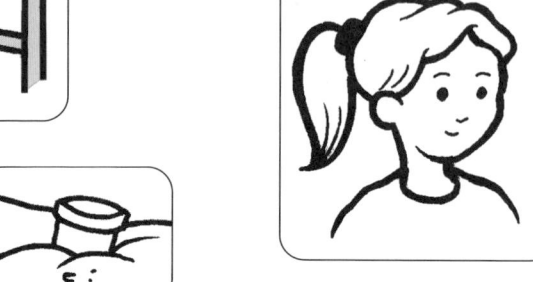

Developing Language Comprehension Using Multisensory Activities
Unit 24 - Picture #2 & Clues

Step 1

Tell your students to look at Picture #1 as you tell them about this picture. They will learn what is happening as they **listen** to you, **look** at the picture and attend as you **point to and touch** the target points in the picture.

> **Example: Look at this picture. You see people at their neighborhood swimming pool. It is a hot summer day. You see Liz, Ben and their dad. They are having fun. You also see a boy relaxing on a chair near the pool. You see a lifeguard sitting on a chair high above the pool. He is on duty. He is watching everyone in the pool. He is there so everyone is safe in the pool. Ben is floating in the pool. Liz is swimming. Dad is diving into the pool.**

Step 2

Next, ask students to tell you about the picture. Ask them to look at the picture and tell you what each person is doing. As you modeled, students should point to and touch a person's face while referring to the person, to the area of the body involved in an action while referring to the action and to the object of an action when referring to the object.

Step 3

Now ask your students to look at Picture #1 and answer these questions.

    Who are the children in the pool?

    Who is diving into the pool?

    Where is the lifeguard?

    What is the lifeguard's job?

    Who is floating? What do you think "floating" means?

    What is Liz doing?

    Is someone relaxing? Where is he?

Step 4

Finally, select one group of questions. Instruct students to look at Picture #2 showing only the swimming pool and answer the questions.

Who were the people in the picture?	Who were the people in the picture?	Who were the people in the picture?
Where were they?	Where were they?	Where were they?
What kind of weather were they having?	What season do you think this was?	Was Ben sinking into the water?
What was Liz doing?	Who was in the pool?	Was Dad swimming?
What was Ben doing?	Where was the lifeguard?	Where were Ben and Liz? What was each of them doing?
Who was sitting in a chair high above the pool?	Where was Dad? What was he doing?	What was the lifeguard doing?
Was someone diving into the pool? Who?	Was someone relaxing? Where was this person?	What would the lifeguard do if someone was having trouble in the pool?
	Who was the lifeguard watching?	

Developing Language Comprehension Using Multisensory Activities
Unit 25 - Picture #1

Developing Language Comprehension Using Multisensory Activities
Unit 25 - Picture #2 & Clues

Step 1

Tell your students to look at Picture #1 as you tell them about this picture. They will learn what is happening as they **listen** to you, **look** at the picture and attend as you **point to and touch** the target points in the picture.

> **Example: Look at this picture. You see three people, Zoe, Tom and their mom. They are at the grocery store. They are shopping for food. Now they are in the cereal aisle. Mom is talking to Tom. She is holding two boxes of cereal. Tom is thinking. He is deciding which cereal to choose. Zoe is waiting for Tom to decide.**

Step 2

Next, ask students to tell you about the picture. Ask them to look at the picture and tell you what each person is doing. As you modeled, students should point to and touch a person's face while referring to the person, to the area of the body involved in an action while referring to the action and to the object of an action when referring to the object.

Step 3

Now ask your students to look at Picture #1 and answer these questions.

Who are the children in this picture?

Who else is in the picture?

Where are these people?

Who is talking to Tom?

What is Mom holding?

What is Tom doing?

What is Zoe doing?

Do you like to decide which cereal to buy at your grocery store?

Step 4

Finally, select one group of questions. Instruct students to look at Picture #2 showing only the grocery store and answer the questions.

Name the children who were in the picture?	**Who were the people in the picture?**	**Who were the people in the picture?**
Which one of their parents was with them?	**In what aisle of the grocery store were they?**	**Where were they?**
Where were they?	**Who was Mom talking to?**	**Who was holding something? What was this?**
Was someone holding something? Who?	**What was Tom doing?**	**Why do you think Mom was holding the boxes?**
Who was talking? What was this person saying?	**What was Zoe doing?**	**What was Tom doing?**
Who was she talking to?	**Do you think Zoe likes to wait?**	**Who was waiting? What was she waiting for?**
Who was waiting?		**What kind of cereal would you choose?**

WHICH ONE
SHOULD I
CHOOSE?

Developing Language Comprehension Using Multisensory Activities
Unit 26 - Picture #2 & Clues

Step 1

Tell your students to look at Picture #1 as you tell them about this picture. They will learn what is happening as they **listen** to you, **look** at the picture and attend as you **point to and touch** the target points in the picture.

> **Example: Look at this picture. You see four children riding on their school bus. Zoe, Liz, Tom and a boy from their neighborhood are on their way home from school. Liz, Zoe and Tom are looking out the window. They see their friend, Beth, outside. Beth is waving to them. Liz is pointing to Beth. Zoe is looking at her out the window and waving. Tom is also looking at Beth and waving to her. All three of these children are surprised and happy to see their friend, Beth.**

Step 2

Next, ask students to tell you about the picture. Ask them to look at the picture and tell you what each child is doing. As you modeled, students should point to and touch a child's face while referring to the child, to the area of the body involved in an action while referring to the action and to the object of an action when referring to the object.

Step 3

Now ask your students to look at Picture #1 and answer these questions.

Where are Liz, Zoe and Tom?

Why are these children on the bus? Where are they going?

Who is pointing? Who is she pointing to?

Who do Tom and Zoe see?

What are Tom and Zoe doing?

Are Tom, Liz and Zoe happy to see their friend, Beth? How do you know?

Step 4

Finally, select one group of questions. Instruct students to look at Picture #2 showing only the school bus and answer the questions.

Can you name three of the children who were on the bus?	**Name three of the children riding the bus.**	**Name three of the children on the bus.**
Where were they?	**Why were Liz, Tom and Zoe on the bus? Where were they going?**	**Tom, Zoe and Liz were riding home. Where were they coming from?**
Liz was looking out the window. Who did she see?	**Was their friend, Beth on the bus too?**	**Was Beth on the bus?**
What were Tom and Zoe doing?	**Who was pointing? Why was she pointing?**	**What was Liz doing?**
What was their friend, Beth doing?	**What were Tom and Zoe doing?**	**Why were Tom and Zoe waving?**
How did Tom, Zoe and Liz feel when they saw Beth outside?	**Did Beth see Liz, Zoe and Tom? How do you know?**	**What was Beth doing?**
		Were Tom, Liz and Zoe surprised to see Beth?

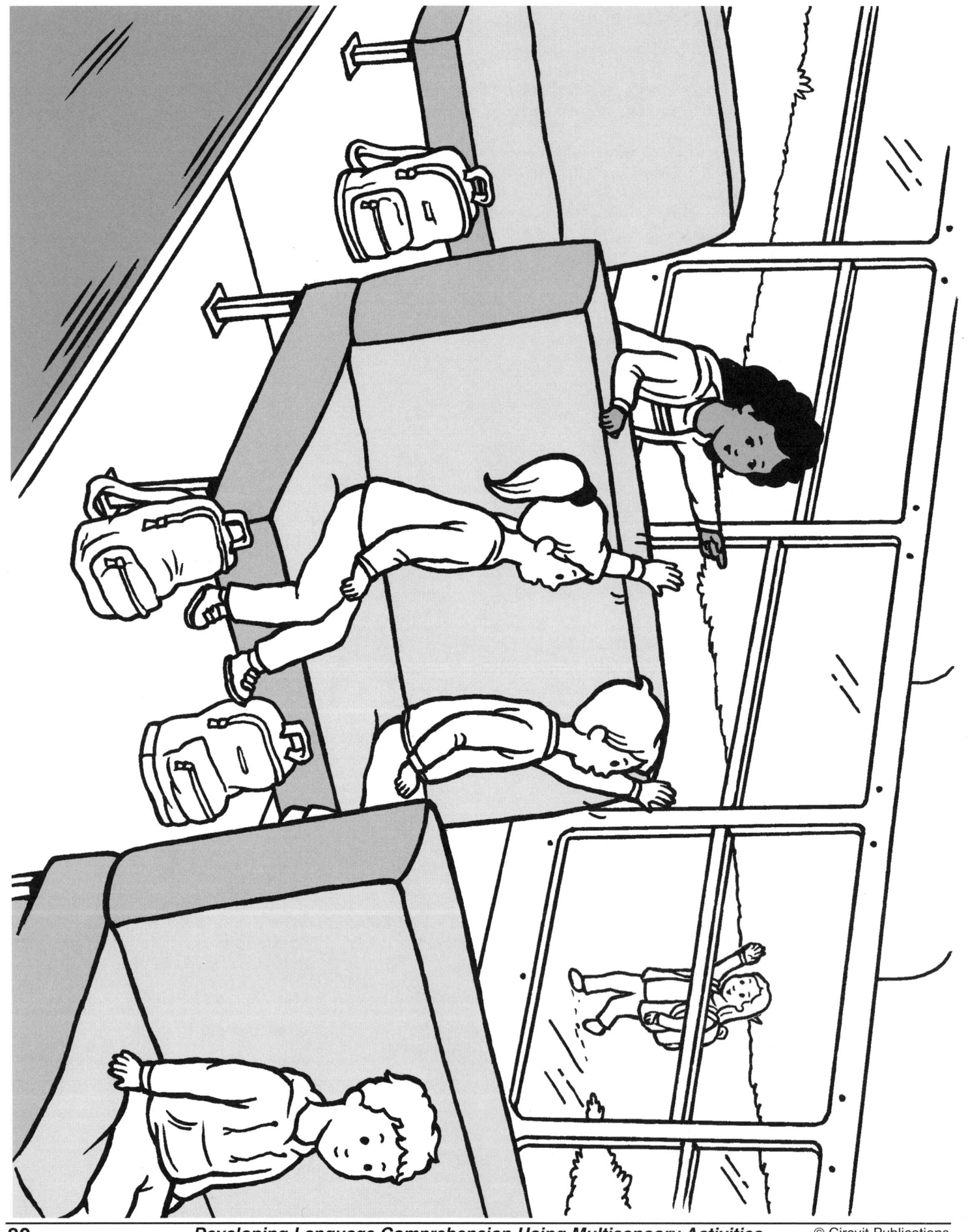

Developing Language Comprehension Using Multisensory Activities
Unit 27 - Picture #1

Developing Language Comprehension Using Multisensory Activities
Unit 27 - Picture #2 & Clues

Step 1

Tell your students to look at Picture #1 as you tell them about this picture. They will learn what is happening as they **listen** to you, **look** at the picture and attend as you **point to and touch** the target points in the picture.

Example: Look at this picture. You see Luke, Cara, some of their classmates and their teacher. Cara is pointing to Luke. Luke is standing in the center of the rug. He is pretending to be a pirate. He is holding a treasure map and showing it to the other children and to the teacher.

Step 2

Next, ask students to tell you about the picture. Ask them to look at the picture and tell you what each person is doing. As you modeled, students should point to and touch a person's face while referring to the person, to the area of the body involved in an action while referring to the action and to the object of an action when referring to the object.

Step 3

Now ask your students to look at Picture #1 and answer these questions.

How many children are in this picture?

Where are they?

Who else is there?

What is Luke pretending to be?

What do pirates search for?

What is Luke holding?

Who is pointing to Luke?

What is the teacher doing?

Step 4

Finally, select one group of questions. Instruct students to look at Picture #2 showing only the preschool classroom and answer the questions.

Who were the people in the picture?	**Who were the people in the picture?**	**Who were the people in the picture?**
Where were they?	**Where were they?**	**Where were they?**
All but one child were sitting on the floor. Which child was not sitting?	**What was Luke pretending?**	**What was Cara pointing to?**
Who was pointing to Luke?	**What was he holding up?**	**On what part of the rug was Luke standing?**
Was Luke in a corner of the rug or in the center?	**What do pirates do with treasure maps?**	**What were the others doing?**
What was Luke doing?	**Did Luke have a real or a pretend treasure map?**	**What was the teacher doing?**
		If Luke was a real pirate what would he do with the treasure map?

Developing Language Comprehension Using Multisensory Activities
Unit 28 - Picture #2 & Clues

Step 1

Tell your students to look at Picture #1 as you tell them about this picture. They will learn what is happening as they **listen** to you, **look** at the picture and attend as you **point to and touch** the target points in the picture.

> **Example: Look at this picture. You see Tom and Zoe. They are cleaning up the playroom. They want their playroom to look neat and clean. You also see their mom. She is helping the children clean up. Mom is using the vacuum cleaner. She is vacuuming the rug in the playroom. Tom is picking up crayons and putting them into a box. Zoe is putting their big blocks away. She is stacking them up.**

Step 2

Next, ask students to tell you about the picture. Ask them to look at the picture and tell you what each person is doing. As you modeled, students should point to and touch a person's face while referring to the person, to the area of the body involved in an action while referring to the action and to the object of an action when referring to the object.

Step 3

Now ask your students to look at Picture #1 and answer these questions.

Who are the children in the picture?

Where are they?

Who is the grown-up in the picture?

What is Mom doing?

Who is putting the crayons away?

What is Zoe doing?

Why are the children and their mom doing these jobs?

Step 4

Finally, select one group of questions. Instruct students to look at Picture #2 showing only the playroom and answer the questions.

Who were the people in the picture? **Where were they?** **Someone was picking up crayons. Who was this?** **Who was stacking blocks?** **What was Mom doing?** **Why was everyone working in the playroom?**	**Can you name the children in the picture?** **Who was the grown-up?** **Where were these people?** **What was Zoe doing with the blocks?** **Where was Tom putting the crayons?** **How do you think the playroom would look when everyone was finished?**	**Who were the people in the picture?** **Where were they?** **What was Zoe's job in the playroom?** **What was Tom's job?** **Mom was working with something that uses electricity. What was this?** **Who was using it?** **Why was everyone working?**

Developing Language Comprehension Using Multisensory Activities
Unit 29 - Picture #1

Step 1

Tell your students to look at Picture #1 as you tell them about this picture. They will learn what is happening as they **listen** to you, **look** at the picture and attend as you **point to and touch** the target points in the picture.

> **Example: Look at this picture. You see three people, Ben, Liz and their mom. They are in Ben's bedroom. They are getting ready to go on a trip. Mom is packing their suitcase. Ben is folding his shirt. Liz is holding her slippers. She will put her slippers into the suitcase so she can bring them on the trip. Mom is putting a sweater into the suitcase.**

Step 2

Next, ask students to tell you about the picture. Ask them to look at the picture and tell you what each person is doing. As you modeled, students should point to and touch a person's face while referring to the person, to the area of the body involved in an action while referring to the action and to the object of an action when referring to the object.

Step 3

Now ask your students to look at Picture #1 and answer these questions.

Name the people who are in this picture.

Where are these people?

What is Mom doing?

What is Ben folding?

What is Liz holding?

Why is Liz holding her slippers?

Step 4

Finally, select one group of questions. Instruct students to look at Picture #2 showing only the bedroom and answer the questions.

Can you name the people in the picture?	**Who were the people in the picture?**	**Name the people in the picture?**
Where were they?	**Where were they?**	**Where were they?**
What were Liz, Ben and Mom getting ready for?	**Why was Mom packing a suitcase?**	**What was Mom putting into the suitcase?**
What was Liz holding?	**What was Mom putting into the suitcase?**	**Why was Ben folding the shirt?**
Who was folding something?	**What was Ben folding?**	**What was Mom doing?**
What was Mom doing?	**What was Liz holding?**	**What would Liz do with her slippers?**
Why do people need suitcases?		

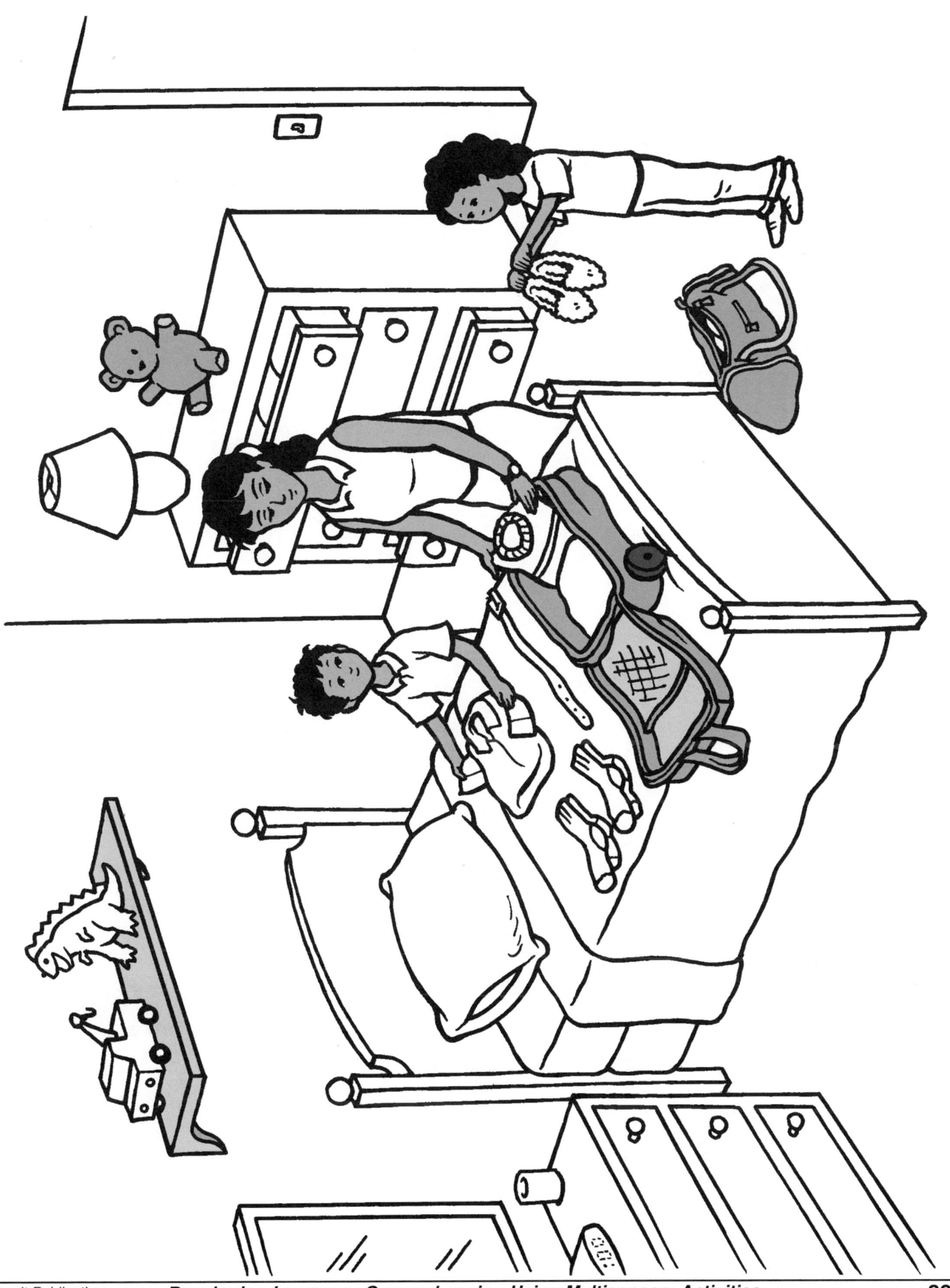

Developing Language Comprehension Using Multisensory Activities
Unit 30 - Picture #1

Developing Language Comprehension Using Multisensory Activities
Unit 30 - Picture #2 & Clues

Step 1

Tell your students to look at Picture #1 as you tell them about this picture. They will learn what is happening as they **listen** to you, **look** at the picture and attend as you **point to and touch** the target points in the picture.

> **Example: Look at this picture. You see two children, Zoe and Tom. They are at the library. Zoe is writing her name so she can get her own library card. A librarian is helping Zoe. She is pointing to the space on Zoe's paper where Zoe should write her name. Tom has already chosen his books to borrow. He is waiting for the librarian to help him check out his books.**

Step 2

Next, ask students to tell you about the picture. Ask them to look at the picture and tell you what each person is doing. As you modeled, students should point to and touch a person's face while referring to the person, to the area of the body involved in an action while referring to the action and to the object of an action when referring to the object.

Step 3

Now ask your students to look at Picture #1 and answer these questions.

Name the children in this picture.

Where are these children?

Who is the grown-up in the picture?

What is Zoe writing?

Why is Zoe writing her name?

Is someone helping Zoe? Who?

What is Tom doing?

Step 4

Finally, select one group of questions. Instruct students to look at Picture #2 showing only the library and answer the questions.

Name the children in this picture.	**Who were the people in this picture?**	**Who were the children in the picture?**
Who else was in the picture?	**Where were they?**	**Who was the adult in the picture?**
Where were these people?	**Who had chosen some books to borrow?**	**Where were these people?**
Was the librarian helping someone? Who?	**Why was the librarian pointing to a space on Zoe's paper?**	**What was the librarian doing to help Zoe?**
The librarian was pointing to something. What was this?	**What was Zoe doing?**	**Who was writing something? What? Why was she doing this?**
What was Tom holding?	**Why was Zoe writing her name?**	**What was Tom doing?**
	What was Tom waiting for?	

Developing Language Comprehension Using Multisensory Activities
Unit 31 - Picture #1

Developing Language Comprehension Using Multisensory Activities
Unit 31 - Picture #2 & Clues

Step 1

Tell your students to look at Picture #1 as you tell them about this picture. They will learn what is happening as they **listen** to you, **look** at the picture and attend as you **point to and touch** the target points in the picture.

> **Example: Look at this picture. You see Ben, Liz, Cara and their mom and dad. They are waiting for Mom to buy their train tickets. Mom is holding money to pay for the tickets. Dad is pulling a suitcase and holding Cara's hand. Ben and Liz are eating popcorn. Ben is sharing his popcorn with Cara.**

Step 2

Next, ask students to tell you about the picture. Ask them to look at the picture and tell you what each person is doing. As you modeled, students should point to and touch a person's face while referring to the person, to the area of the body involved in an action while referring to the action and to the object of an action when referring to the object.

Step 3

Now ask your students to look at Picture #1 and answer these questions.

Who do you see in this picture?

Where are these people?

Why do you think Mom is buying train tickets?

What is Dad doing?

Who is eating popcorn?

Who is sharing popcorn with someone? With whom?

Step 4

Finally, select one group of questions. Instruct students to look at Picture #2 showing only the train station and answer the questions.

Who did you see in the picture?	**Who were the people in the picture?**	**Who were the people in the picture?**
Where were they?	**Where were they?**	**Where were they?**
Who was buying train tickets?	**What was Mom doing?**	**Who was buying tickets?**
What was Dad pulling?	**What were Liz and Ben doing?**	**Who was holding someone's hand?**
What were Ben and Liz eating?	**Who was sharing popcorn?**	**Who was standing in line?**
What was Mom holding? What was this for?	**What was Dad pulling?**	**Who was taking some of Ben's popcorn?**
Was someone getting off the train?	**Why do you think this family was at the train station?**	**What would probably happen after Mom got the tickets?**

Developing Language Comprehension Using Multisensory Activities
Unit 32 - Picture #1

Developing Language Comprehension Using Multisensory Activities

Unit 32 - Picture #2 & Clues

Step 1

Tell your students to look at Picture #1 as you tell them about this picture. They will learn what is happening as they **listen** to you, **look** at the picture and attend as you **point to and touch** the target points in the picture.

> **Example: Look at this picture. You see five people. Tom and Zoe, their mom and dad, and their little brother, Luke. They are camping in the woods. Mom is setting up the tent. She is pounding a tent peg into the ground. Tom is helping Mom. He is holding more tent pegs for her. Dad is building their campfire. He is putting a stick on the fire. Zoe is helping Dad. She is holding another stick for the fire. Luke is helping too. He is carrying a big log for the fire.**

Step 2

Next, ask students to tell you about the picture. Ask them to look at the picture and tell you what each person is doing. As you modeled, students should point to and touch a person's face while referring to the person, to the area of the body involved in an action while referring to the action and to the object of an action when referring to the object.

Step 3

Now ask your students to look at Picture #1 and answer these questions.

Name the people in this picture.

Where are these people?

What is Mom doing? How do you think a tent gets set up?

Who is helping Mom?

What is Dad doing? How do you think a campfire is built?

What is Luke carrying?

What is Zoe holding?

Step 4

Finally, select one group of questions. Instruct students to look at Picture #2 showing only the campground and answer the questions.

Who were the children in this picture?	**You saw five people in the picture. Who were they?**	**Who were the people in the picture?**
Who were the adults?	**Where was this family?**	**Where were they?**
Where were these people?	**Who was building a fire? Who was helping?**	**Two people were working on the tent. Who were they?**
Who was setting up the tent? Who was helping?	**What was Zoe doing to help Dad with the fire?**	**What do you think the tent would be used for?**
What was Tom holding?		**Who was building the campfire? Who was helping?**
What was Dad doing?	**What was Luke carrying?**	**Why do you need campfires?**
Luke was carrying a big log. What was this for?	**What was Mom pounding?**	**Why must campers be careful when building fires?**
What was Zoe holding?	**Who was helping Mom?**	

Developing Language Comprehension Using Multisensory Activities
Unit 33 - Picture #1

Developing Language Comprehension Using Multisensory Activities
Unit 33 - Picture #2 & Clues

Step 1

Tell your students to look at Picture #1 as you tell them about this picture. They will learn what is happening as they **listen** to you, **look** at the picture and attend as you **point to and touch** the target points in the picture.

Example: Look at this picture. You see Ben and Liz. They are in their doctor's office. They are getting checked by the doctor. You also see their doctor and nurse. Everyone is doing something. Ben is standing on the doctor's scale. The doctor is weighing and measuring Ben to see how much he weighs and how tall he is. The nurse is writing notes about Ben. He is writing how tall Ben is. Liz is standing next to the nurse. She is waiting for her turn to be weighed and measured.

Step 2

Next, ask students to tell you about the picture. Ask them to look at the picture and tell you what each person is doing. As you modeled, students should point to and touch a person's face while referring to the person, to the area of the body involved in an action while referring to the action and to the object of an action when referring to the object.

Step 3

Now ask your students to look at Picture #1 and answer these questions.

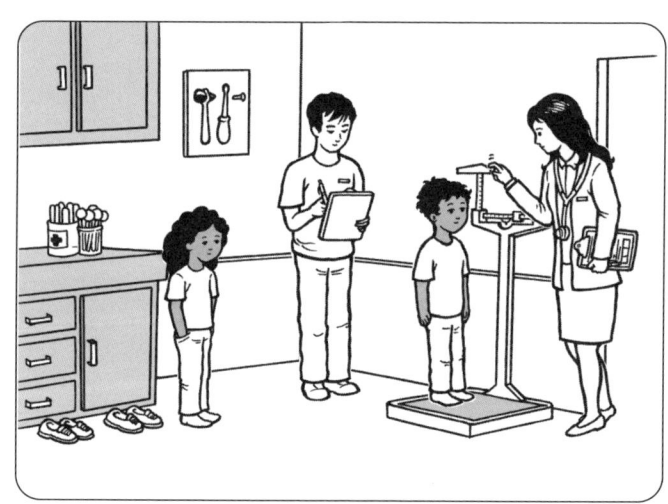

Who are the people in this picture?

Where are they?

Where is Ben standing? Why is he standing there?

What is the doctor doing?

What is the nurse doing?

What is Liz waiting for?

Step 4

Finally, select one group of questions. Instruct students to look at Picture #2 showing only the doctor's office and answer the questions.

Who were the people in the picture?	**Name the children in the picture.**	**Who were the people in the picture?**
Where were these people?	**Who were the grown-ups in the picture?**	**Where were they?**
Was the doctor weighing and measuring someone? Who was this?	**Where were these people?**	**Why were Liz and Ben at their doctor's office?**
Was someone writing notes? Who was this?	**Where was Ben standing?**	**What was Liz waiting for?**
Who was he writing about?	**What was the doctor doing?**	**What was the doctor doing?**
Do you know how much you weigh?	**Who was writing something?**	**What was the nurse doing?**
	What was Liz doing?	**Do you know how tall you are?**

Developing Language Comprehension Using Multisensory Activities
Unit 34 - Picture #1

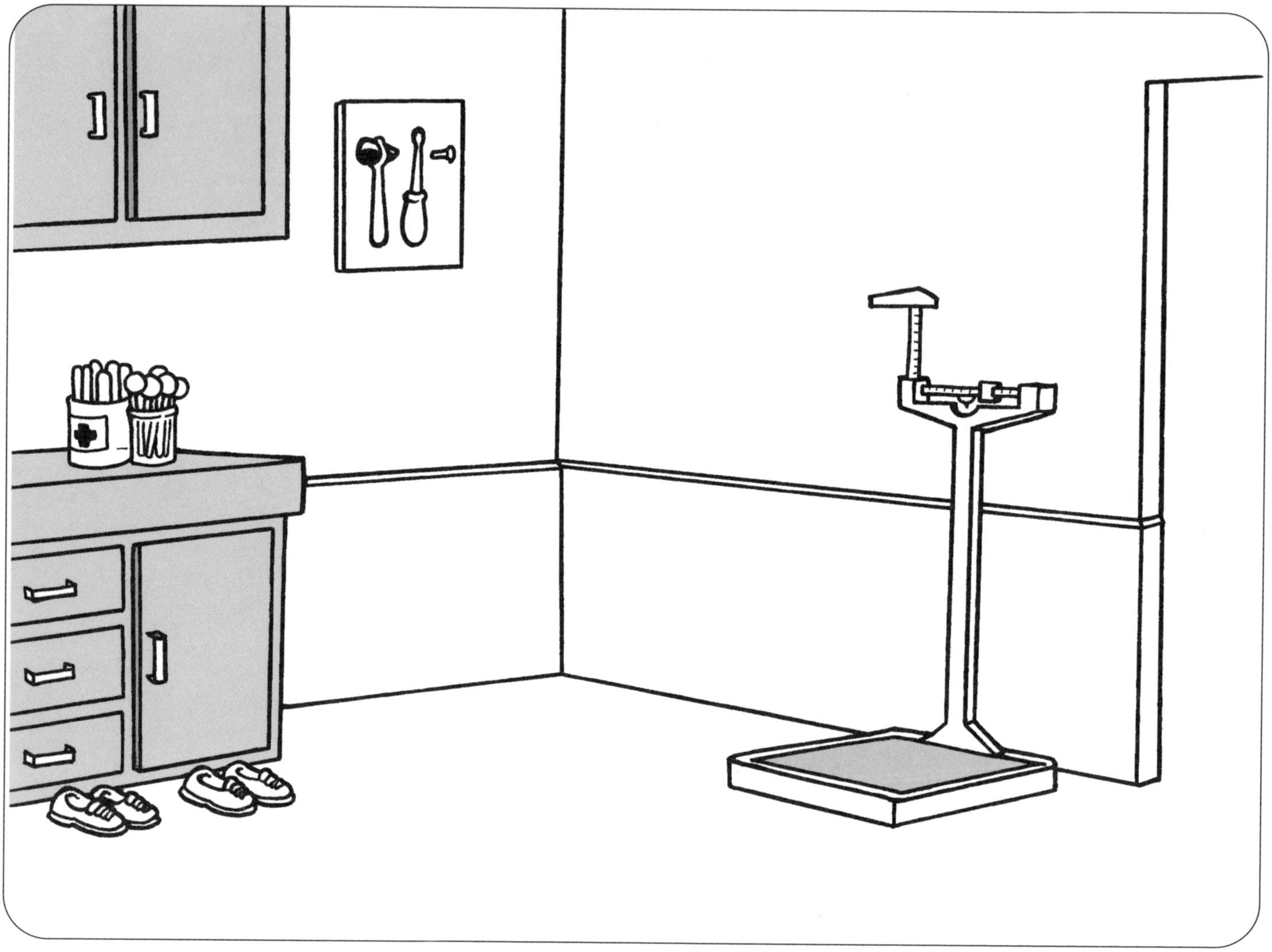

Developing Language Comprehension Using Multisensory Activities
Unit 34 - Picture #2 & Clues

Step 1

Tell your students to look at Picture #1 as you tell them about this picture. They will learn what is happening as they **listen** to you, **look** at the picture and attend as you **point to and touch** the target points in the picture.

> **Example: Look at this picture. You see Zoe, her brother, Tom and some of their friends. They are at a party celebrating Zoe's birthday. Zoe is unwrapping a present while her friends watch. Zoe's friend, Liz is helping her. She is holding a present for Zoe to open next. Tom is helping Zoe too. He is holding a big trash bag for papers and ribbons.**

Step 2

Next, ask students to tell you about the picture. Ask them to look at the picture and tell you what each child is doing. As you modeled, students should point to and touch a child's face while referring to the child, to the area of the body involved in an action while referring to the action and to the object of an action when referring to the object.

Step 3

Now ask your students to look at Picture #1 and answer these questions.

Name some of the children in this picture.

What are they celebrating?

Where are they?

What is Zoe doing??

What is Zoe's brother, Tom, doing?

Who is holding the next present that Zoe will open?

Why do people celebrate birthdays?

Step 4

Finally, select one group of questions. Instruct students to look at Picture #2 showing only the party room and answer the questions.

Name three children who were at Zoe's party. **What was everyone celebrating at this party?** **What was Zoe doing?** **What was Tom holding?** **What was this for?** **What was Liz holding?** **Who was watching Zoe?**	**You saw a picture of someone's birthday party. Whose party was this?** **Who was opening a present?** **Who was holding a trash bag?** **Were the children eating something?** **What happened to the papers and ribbons after the presents were opened?**	**Who were the children in this picture?** **Where were these children?** **What were Zoe's friends doing in the picture?** **Two people were helping Zoe. Who were they?** **How was Liz helping Zoe?** **How was Tom helping?** **What do you do to celebrate birthdays?**

Developing Language Comprehension Using Multisensory Activities
Unit 35 - Picture #1

Step 1

Tell your students to look at Picture #1 as you tell them about this picture. They will learn what is happening as they **listen** to you, **look** at the picture and attend as you **point to and touch** the target points in the picture.

> **Example: Look at this picture. You see Tom, Zoe, Luke and their mom and dad. This family is on an airplane. Dad is in the seat behind Tom. Luke is in the seat behind Mom. The family is going to visit the children's grandparents who live in another city. Everyone is waiting for the plane to take off. Tom is buckling his seat belt. Zoe is in the seat next to Tom. Her seat belt is already buckled. She is playing a game. Mom's seat belt is buckled and she is holding everyone's plane tickets. In the next row Dad is buckling Luke's seat belt.**

Step 2

Next, ask students to tell you about the picture. Ask them to look at the picture and tell you what each person is doing. As you modeled, students should point to and touch a person's face while referring to the person, to the area of the body involved in an action while referring to the action and to the object of an action when referring to the object.

Step 3

Now ask your students to look at Picture #1 and answer these questions.

> **Name the people in Zoe and Tom's family who are in the picture.**
>
> **Where are they?**
>
> **What is everyone waiting for?**
>
> **What is Zoe doing?**
>
> **Whose seat belts are not yet buckled?**
>
> **Who is buckling his own seat belt?**

Step 4

Finally, select one group of questions. Instruct students to look at Picture #2 showing only the airplane and answer the questions.

Who were the people that you know in the picture? **Where were they?** **Where were they going?** **What were they waiting for?** **What was Tom doing?** **Who was helping Luke?** **Why do people wear seat belts when they ride on airplanes?**	**Who were the people in this family?** **Where were they?** **What was Mom holding?** **Who was playing a game?** **Someone was buckling his own seat belt. Who was this?** **Who needed help to buckle his seat belt?** **Who was holding everyone's plane tickets?**	**Name the people you know in this picture?** **Where were they?** **Why were they on an airplane?** **What was Mom doing?** **What would happen soon?** **What was Zoe doing?** **Who was helping Luke buckle his seat belt?**

Developing Language Comprehension Using Multisensory Activities
Unit 36 - Picture #1

Developing Language Comprehension Using Multisensory Activities
Unit 36 - Picture #2 & Clues

Step 1

Tell your students to look at Picture #1 as you tell them about this picture. They will learn what is happening as they **listen** to you, **look** at the picture and attend as you **point to and touch** the target points in the picture.

> **Example: Look at this picture. You see Tom, Zoe, Luke and their mom. They are at the library. Zoe is holding a book she wants to borrow. She is choosing another book from the shelf. Tom is deciding which DVD he want s to borrow. Luke and Mom are standing near the aquarium. Luke is showing Mom a book about fish. Mom is telling Luke that they can take that book home.**

Step 2

Next, ask students to tell you about the picture. Ask them to look at the picture and tell you what each person is doing. As you modeled, students should point to and touch a person's face while referring to the person, to the area of the body involved in an action while referring to the action and to the object of an action when referring to the object.

Step 3

Now ask your students to look at Picture #1 and answer these questions.

    Who are the people in this picture?

    Where are they?

    What is Tom deciding?

    What is Zoe holding?

    Where are Luke and Mom standing?

    What are they talking about?

Step 4

Finally, select one group of questions. Instruct students to look at Picture #2 showing only the library and answer the questions.

Who were the people in the picture?	**Who were the people in the picture?**	**Who were the people in the picture?**
Where were they?	**Where were they?**	**Where were they?**
What was Zoe holding?	**What was Tom deciding?**	**What was Zoe holding? What else was she doing?**
What was Luke showing Mom?	**What was inside the aquarium?**	**Was Tom ready to leave?**
What was Mom telling Luke?	**Was Luke interested in fish? Why do you think so?**	**Who was Luke talking to?**
Did Tom know which DVD he wanted?	**What was Zoe choosing?**	**What were they talking about?**
		Were Luke and Mom sitting at a table?

Developing Language Comprehension Using Multisensory Activities
Unit 37 - Picture #1

Developing Language Comprehension Using Multisensory Activities
Unit 37 - Picture #2 & Clues

Step 1

Tell your students to look at Picture #1 as you tell them about this picture. They will learn what is happening as they **listen** to you, **look** at the picture and attend as you **point to and touch** the target points in the picture.

> **Example: Look at this picture. You see Tom, Zoe, their little brother, Luke and their dad. They are having fun at the beach. You also see their friend, Ben. Zoe is kneeling in the sand collecting sea shells. She is putting the shells in a pail. Tom and Ben are throwing a beach ball to each other. Ben threw the ball. Tom is ready to catch it. Dad is relaxing on the beach. Luke is sitting near him. Dad and Luke are watching Tom and Ben.**

Step 2

Next, ask students to tell you about the picture. Ask them to look at the picture and tell you what each person is doing. As you modeled, students should point to and touch a person's face while referring to the person, to the area of the body involved in an action while referring to the action and to the object of an action when referring to the object.

Step 3

Now ask your students to look at Picture #1 and answer these questions.

Who are the people in this picture?

Where are these people?

What are Tom and Ben doing?

What is Zoe collecting?

Someone is relaxing. Who is this?

Where is Luke sitting?

Is anyone watching Ben and Tom?

Step 4

Finally, select one group of questions. Instruct students to look at Picture #2 showing only the beach and answer the questions.

Who were the people that you saw in the picture?	**Can you name the people who were in the picture?**	**Who were the people in the picture?**
Where were these people?	**Where were these people?**	**Where were these people?**
Who was collecting sea shells?	**What time of year do you think this was? Why do you think so?**	**What was Zoe doing?**
Who was throwing a ball?	**Who was kneeling?**	**What was Dad doing?**
Who was ready to catch the ball?	**What were Tom and Ben playing with?**	**What was Luke doing?**
Who was relaxing?	**Who were Luke and Dad watching?**	**Where did Zoe put the shells that she found?**
Who was sitting near Dad?	**What was Zoe collecting?**	**What were Ben and Tom doing?**
		Who was watching Ben and Tom play with the ball?

Developing Language Comprehension Using Multisensory Activities
Unit 38 - Picture #2 & Clues

Step 1

Tell your students to look at Picture #1 as you tell them about this picture. They will learn what is happening as they **listen** to you, **look** at the picture and attend as you **point to and touch** the target points in the picture.

> **Example: Look at this picture. You see Tom, Zoe, their mom and dad and their little brother, Luke. They are at a party store. Mom and Dad are holding shopping bags. Tom is doing something that is making everyone laugh. He is putting on a silly mask. Mom and Dad are looking at Tom. They are laughing. Zoe is looking at Tom. She is laughing too. Zoe is holding Luke's hand. Luke is pointing to Tom and laughing.**

Step 2

Next, ask students to tell you about the picture. Ask them to look at the picture and tell you what each person is doing. As you modeled, students should point to and touch a person's face while referring to the person, to the area of the body involved in an action while referring to the action and to the object of an action when referring to the object.

Step 3

Now ask your students to look at Picture #1 and answer these questions.

> Name the people who are in this picture.
>
> Where are they?
>
> How is Tom making everyone laugh?
>
> Two people are holding shopping bags. Who are they?
>
> Who is pointing to Tom?
>
> Who is holding Luke's hand?

Step 4

Finally, select one group of questions. Instruct students to look at Picture #2 showing only the party store and answer the questions.

Who were the people in the picture?	Who were the people in this the picture?	Who were the people in this the picture?
Where were these people?	Where was this family?	Where was this family?
What was Tom doing?	Two people were holding shopping bags. Who were they?	Who was Luke pointing to?
Why do you think Tom was trying on the silly mask?	Who was holding Luke's hand?	Who was not laughing?
Who was laughing?	Who was making everyone laugh?	Why were people laughing?
Who was holding Luke's hand?	What are some things that might be sold at a party store?	How do you know that Mom and Dad had probably been shopping?
What were Mom and Dad holding?		

Developing Language Comprehension Using Multisensory Activities
Unit 39 - Picture #1

Step 1

Tell your students to look at Picture #1 as you tell them about this picture. They will learn what is happening as they **listen** to you, **look** at the picture and attend as you **point to and touch** the target points in the picture.

Example: Look at this picture. You see Ben, Tom and their teacher. They are in their classroom. You also see three of their classmates, two boys and one girl. Tom and Ben are sitting at a table. Tom is reading and Ben is writing on a paper. Their classmates are standing. One boy is writing numbers on the board. The other boy is feeding their classroom pet, a hamster. The girl is standing by a table and watering a plant.

Step 2

Next, ask students to tell you about the picture. Ask them to look at the picture and tell you what each person is doing. As you modeled, students should point to and touch a person's face while referring to the person, to the area of the body involved in an action while referring to the action and to the object of an action when referring to the object.

Step 3

Now ask your students to look at Picture #1 and answer these questions.

Who are the boys sitting at the table?

What is Ben doing?

What is Tom doing?

You see three of their classmates. How many are boys? How many are girls?

Who is feeding the classroom pet?

What kind of animal is this?

Is a girl writing numbers on the board?

Step 4

Finally, select one group of questions. Instruct students to look at Picture #2 showing only the classroom and answer the questions.

How many children did you see in the picture?	How many children were in the classroom? Who were they?	Name the two boys who you know.
Where were Ben and Tom?	Who was reading?	Who else was in the picture?
Who was reading? Who was writing on paper?	What was Ben doing?	Where were they?
Were Tom and Ben's classmates sitting or standing?	Were Ben and Tom sitting at their desks?	What was Tom doing?
Was a girl feeding the pet hamster?	Was a boy drawing a picture on the board?	What was Ben doing?
What was someone writing on the board?	What was the girl doing?	Who was watering a plant, a boy or a girl?
Was a boy watering the plant?	What was the classroom pet?	How many boys were writing something on the board?

Developing Language Comprehension Using Multisensory Activities
Unit 40 - Picture #1

Developing Language Comprehension Using Multisensory Activities
Unit 40 - Picture #2 & Clues